The Story of Tattersalls

Also by Peter Willett

Makers of the Modern Thoroughbred
The Classic Racehorse
An Introduction to the Thoroughbred

The Story of Tattersalls

Peter Willett

Stanley Paul
London Melbourne Auckland Johannesburg

Stanley Paul & Co. Ltd

An imprint of Century Hutchinson Ltd

62–65 Chandos Place, London WC2N 4NW

Century Hutchinson Australia (Pty) Ltd
PO Box 496, 16–22 Church Street, Hawthorn,
Melbourne, Victoria 3122

Century Hutchinson New Zealand Limited
PO Box 40–086, Glenfield, Auckland 10

Century Hutchinson South Africa (Pty) Ltd
PO Box 337, Bergvlei 2012, South Africa

First published 1987

Set in 11/13 point Linotron Bembo by Deltatype, Ellesmere Port

Printed and bound in Great Britain by Anchor Brendon Ltd, Tiptree, Essex

ISBN 0 09 171290 4

CONTENTS

Foreword

Even before I took over from my cousin, Ken, as chairman of Tattersalls, I had planned that we should commission a new history of the firm. The original book, written after the war by Vincent Orchard, was somewhat prosaic and also incomplete, as it failed to give a full picture of the years between the wars when 'Mr Sommy', Gerald Deane, Bob Needham and latterly my father were in control, and of course it did not take the story up to the present day.

Having made this decision, Tattersalls approached Peter Willett to write the book, and to our delight he accepted. A scholar of renown and accomplishment and already the author of several books on closely allied subjects, Peter Willett has exhaustively researched the subject and provided us with an unusually well-informed and entertaining history.

I hope that readers will greatly enjoy *The Story of Tattersalls*. I myself think it is fit to be ranked alongside those two outstanding books on the Turf, *Men and Horses I Have Kown* by George Lambton and *Memories of Racing and Hunting* by the late Duke of Portland, the owner of St Simon – sold as a two-year-old by Tattersalls!

Michael Watt
Newmarket, 1987

Introduction

Vincent Orchard's book *Tattersalls* was published in 1953. It described the history of the Tattersall family and the evolution of the auctioneering business that bore their name from the earliest days up to the death of Somerville (Sommy) Tattersall, the last Tattersall to be a member of the firm, in 1942. This volume continues the story of Tattersalls up to the present day.

So the primary purpose of this book is to provide a sequel to Orchard's. But that statement is an oversimplification, for two main reasons. Firstly it is desirable that any history of Tattersalls should include some account of the earlier, formative times in which a great family firm was founded and developed to attain a commanding position in the world of bloodstock sales which has been consolidated and extended in the second half of the twentieth century; for this reason Part One of this book is a condensed version of Orchard's history, though it incorporates some new material and a number of corrections and reappraisals. Secondly, Orchard was too close in time to Sommy Tattersall and his partners Gerald Deane and Robert Needham to be able to assess their personalities and their contributions in the comprehensive manner that is fitting to a history of the firm; the chapter 'The Personalities in the First Half of the Twentieth Century' helps fill this void.

Consequently the present book is a microcosm, a lineal descendant and an extension of Vincent Orchard's *Tattersalls*, which remains, and probably always will remain, the definitive history of the first century and a half of the world's greatest and most long-lived bloodstock auction house.

The author wishes to thank the Directors and Staff of Tattersalls for their essential cooperation in assembling material for this book; Mrs Angela Thorne, Mrs Cecil McCullough, Sir Yehudi Menuhin, Sir John Astor and Mr Geoffrey Hart for supplying much useful information; Mr Patrick Saward for permission to use some of the fruits of his own research; and the late Mr Michael Seth-Smith for valuable assistance in the work of condensing Vincent Orchard's *Tattersalls* during the last months of his life.

The publishers would like to thank Laurie Morton, The Photo Source, Press Association and All-Sport for permission to reproduce copyright photographs.

Part One

Tattersalls and the Tattersall Family

ORIGINALLY the Tattersall family owned property in Brerecliff and Burnley in Lancashire, with records and chronicles tracing their ancestry to Richard Tattersall, who was born in 1444. During his lifetime the Wars of the Roses were fought, with the House of York eventually replacing the House of Lancaster, but there is no evidence that he was involved in the conflict. Five generations later Richard Tattersall's descendant, Edmund, was born at Ridge End, a solid but unpretentious house to the north-east of the straggling village of Burnley. As a young man of almost thirty his ardent loyalty to the Jacobite cause of the Old Pretender cost him dear, and his wife, Ann Varley, whom he had married in 1714, was frightened for his life. Many of his acquaintances were heavily penalized after the battle of Preston, which virtually put paid to the rebellion, and perhaps it was only by good fortune that he escaped similar punishment. However, he deemed it wise to move to a smaller home at Hurstwood, an adjoining village, and is entitled to be acknowledged as the first member of the Tattersall family to be a significant influence upon the history of bloodstock auctioneering, as the father of Richard Tattersall. He and his wife became the parents of six children, three sons and three daughters, of whom Richard was the second. A year younger than his brother John, and born in 1724, Richard was destined to become the founder of the illustrious firm which bore his surname.

He spent the first ten years of his life at Hurstwood before being sent to the Grammar School at Burnley, where he was one of forty boys under the charge of Ellis Nutter, a scholarly man who enforced rigid discipline, and an ancestress of whom had married a Tattersall in 1684. The education that Richard received at the Grammar School was first-class, but he was happier during the school holidays, when he helped his father on the farm and rode with him to local markets and fairs. One day soon after his fourteenth birthday he bought a horse, not apparently a horse of any great quality, but nevertheless one which had seen better days before being used to pull a cart.

Richard hid his new treasure in a disused byre, making expeditions to feed and water him under cover of night. To keep and ride him without discovery was no easy task even for a resourceful boy, and he soon gave himself away. Edmund saw a strange horse and rider on the moor one morning, rode across to investigate, and the secret was out. That evening he talked matters over with his wife. Sentence was promulgated next morning, in a form which his son had certainly not expected. He was given three months in which to decide whether he should work for a scholarship to Cambridge or be apprenticed to a friend of his father, who was a wool-stapler. Neither prospect was particularly attractive to a boy of fourteen and, as Richard's mother was in no hurry to lose him, a compromise was eventually arrived at. He should stay with Mr Nutter until he was sixteen and should then go to the stapler.

Richard was fond of his home, and in the end agreed. Home life, after all, had its compensations. In the holidays, life was spent on the farm, with occasional visits, in the company of his father and brother, to local race meetings, of which at the time there was no lack. Richard himself was no great horseman, but watching horses and especially racehorses was as much a preoccupation to him as farming was to his father.

His apprenticeship to his father's wool-stapling friend did not last long, for Richard had no heart for his allotted tasks, even though the wool trade was the greatest industry in England next to agriculture. By the middle of the eighteenth century the West Riding of Yorkshire was ousting the counties of South-West England and Norfolk from their former supremacy, and John Kay's invention of the flying shuttle in 1733 vastly increased the rapidity of weaving. If he had remained in the wool trade Richard Tattersall might have made a fortune, but he did not elect to do so, deciding instead to go to London. This decision, of which his father approved, may have been influenced by events which occurred in the summer and autumn of 1745.

Bonnie Prince Charlie landed at Eriskay on 23 July and by mid-November had reached Carlisle. During these months young Richard Tattersall had been conscripted to drill with Jacobite supporters under the command of Colonel Francis Towneley on a moor close to Hurstwood, but he had no enthusiasm for the cause. The defeat of the Young Pretender at the bloody battle of Culloden in April 1746 strengthened Richard Tattersall's resolve to travel south, for he and his father believed that the collapse of the Jacobite rebellion heralded another era of prosperity similar to that enjoyed for more than twenty years under the ministry of Sir Robert Walpole. This prosperity was being built up by coal-owners, iron-masters and factory owners and those merchants whose ships brought overseas trade to the docks which lined the banks of the Thames above Greenwich. London was the place for an ambitious young man.

Little is known of Richard's early months in London. He was obviously a presentable young man with a little money provided by his father, but equally he was not a member of any of the fashionable clubs of the era. He found pleasure, however, in attending sales of horses, especially at Hyde Park Corner, and wrote home to his father describing the scene. He also wrote to his father giving details of a lucrative visit to Scotland. He had heard that a Scottish nobleman intended to sell his stud. Richard applied to a friend to go halves in its purchase; the friend agreed and Richard journeyed north. He bought the stud cheaply and sold the stock in York and London for a considerable profit.

About the middle of the century a number of horse auction houses with regular sales days began to develop. The senior establishment appears to have been Beevor's, which in the 1770s became Aldridges, who conducted their business at premises in St Martin's Lane. Mr Beevor's Repository was founded in 1753, its proprietor concentrating mainly on the sale of carriages and carriage horses, hacks, working horses and hunters. It was here that Richard spent his early years in London, and it was here that he suffered his first serious loss. He was head ostler at Beevor's, when one day a thief walked into his bedroom, and departed with his bed and bedding. No one made any attempt to detain him; it was assumed that he was employed by Richard.

After leaving Beevor's, where he believed he had little future, he became stud groom to the Duke of Kingston, who was a member of the Jockey Club, a brother of the celebrated Lady Mary Wortley Montague, and the owner of houses in the fashionable West End of London and at Newmarket in addition to his family seat at Thoresby, in the heart of Sherwood Forest. The Duke interfered little in Richard's performance of his duties, which gave him ample opportunity not only to gain an insight into the world of bloodstock breeding, but also to appreciate the importance and affluence of those who were attempting to organize horse-racing into some semblance of rule and order.

In 1756 Richard married Catherine Somerville, a granddaughter of the 12th Earl of Somerville – an indication that he was accepted in upper-class society. Two years later their son was born; he was christened Edmund, and was to be their only child. At the same time Richard was drawing up ambitious plans for his career with horses. He was popular, enjoyed the patronage of men of the status of the royal Duke of Cumberland, the Duke of Kingston and Earl Grosvenor, and had an enviable reputation for integrity and business ability. The death of his father in 1764 strengthened his resolve to pursue his plans, and his dream of building his own Repository and affording facilities for everyone who wished to buy or sell horses came a step closer to reality.

At that time Hyde Park Corner was the morning rendezvous of fashionable London, and Richard had long set his eyes upon the broad expanse of the Five Fields which lay to the south-east of it. Luckily Lord Grosvenor was careless of this seemingly unimportant portion of his property. 'Say what you want, Tattersall,' he told him, 'and go to see my agents; I will instruct them to give you all the help they can.' More than a century later *Baily's Magazine* (April 1898) printed a long description of eighteenth-century Hyde Park Corner and the vicinity:

To any good judge of the value of London's property, a ninety-nine years' lease of such a piece of ground as the old 'Corner' stood upon, must have seemed worth a big sum of money. Every great capital pushes onwards to the West, where its most fashionable quarters always establish themselves. There must have been a lack of foresight in Lord Grosvenor when he parted, in exchange for a comparatively small rent, with a valuable site for so long a term, unless he did so from personal partiality for his tenant.

In 1766 there was in Hyde Park Corner and its surroundings little to lead frequenters of that lonely and unsightly spot to anticipate what it would be like a century later. In the middle of last century, neither St George's Hospital, nor Apsley House, was built or thought of; the gates and iron screen erected by Decimus Burton to shut off Hyde Park from Piccadilly were not erected until 1825; an old-fashioned turnpike road, which in wet weather was often impassable, except at a foot's pace, to stage-coaches and posting carriages, skirted the southern side of Kensington Gardens and Hyde Park, and nearly in front of the site now occupied by the Alexandra Hotel, a massive turnpike gate stood. It was often the scene of brawls and fights, especially in electioneering times; and when a post-chaise drew up there in the middle of the night, high words often passed between the travellers inside and the sturdy custodian, who kept the chaise waiting so long that he was more than suspected of being in league with the 'gentlemen of the road', of whom there was no lack upon every highway leading to the Metropolis. 'Galloping Dick', 'Seven-stringed Jack', 'Gentleman Foster' and a score or more members of the same exciting profession, stopped everything on wheels that came within their ken, and were especially on the look-out for country gentlemen like Sir Watkin Williams Wynn, who brought their rents up to London in their own carriages twice a year, to deposit them with their London bankers. On the spot where Apsley House now stands, the 'Pillars of Hercules' – a popular tavern, which received this singular name from being regarded as the last House in the West End – opened its doors wide to admit customers, as it did to Squire Western and his fair daughter in Fielding's novel, *Tom Jones*, and also, it was whispered, to several crack highwaymen. Where Belgrave Square, Eaton Square and the fashionable streets in their neighbourhood are now covered with costly aristocratic mansions, a dreary morass, frequented by wild waterfowl and snipe in winter and called the 'Five Fields', gave little presage of what it would grow into before the death of George IV.

No doubt Grosvenor thought he could well afford to part with a portion of such a property. If Tattersall liked to build upon it, so much the better. He could be relied on to protect his stables and barns; the place would be all the safer for decent people. Richard, however, was a cautious person. The development of the Five Fields was no concern of his; in any event he sought only a modest site. He visualized a row of stables, a few kennels, an exercise yard and an auction ring and offices. The place, moreover, should be near the Corner and as

Richard Tattersall (1724–1795), the founder of the firm. From the painting by Thomas Beach

far away as possible from the 'Bloody Bridge'. This venerable institution, once a plank across the Westbourne, where it flowed south by what is now Sloane Square, had been converted into a brick structure by Charles II. It had thus obtained a certain popularity among travellers, and especially among the footpads who robbed and murdered them as they crossed it.

Tattersall, who planned one day to build a home for Catherine and little Edmund, inclined rather to the north side of the Five Fields. The Kensington Road certainly had its disadvantages, but the robbers there at least robbed their victims in a gentlemanly fashion and refrained whenever possible from shooting them.

There was also, in the vicinity of Lanesborough House, a cosy little establishment known as the Turf Tavern. It stood at the bottom of a deep enclosure entered by a small archway from Grosvenor Place, and was the rendezvous of the sporting fraternity. Richard rode round and round the fields but could find nothing he liked better than this pleasant spot. 'My Lord', he told Grosvenor, 'if I may use this little piece of your land, I will be greatly obliged to you'; and Grosvenor was happy to grant him a 99-year lease.

Tattersall was in no hurry to build. His immediate need was to have an office of his own and to adapt the existing boxes and yard to his requirements. He also found that two brothers, one a speculative builder and the other a bricklayer, were in the field before him. They already held leases from Lord Grosvenor of some of the land which Richard coveted. His first move, therefore, was to come to an agreement with the proprietor of the tavern.

There was plenty of room for exercising horses in the adjacent fields, there were the existing stables and, as for offices, the landlord had promised him the sole use of the parlour for two days a week – Mondays and Thursdays. Meanwhile he looked around for a builder. It would be convenient to have a row of boxes of his own.

Since the sales at The Corner took place on only two of the week's six working days, Richard was able to get into the country fairly often, looking for new business and extending his connections. He was by no means without rivals, especially at Newmarket, where the diligent Mr Pond, the compiler of the *Kalendar*, had established himself some twenty years previously. John Pond had already forgotten more about racing than Tattersall had begun to learn, and was a Newmarket man. To what extent he conducted bloodstock auction sales is not clear, but he died in 1768 and Richard took over his vacant pitch or rostrum shortly afterwards.

No one questioned that Richard Tattersall's financial dealings and obligations were carried out with scrupulous honesty – a quality which earned for him an ever-increasing prestige. Moreover, it was a prestige established among the right people. It seemed that at last the Turf had produced a gentleman dealer of unfailing rectitude.

Richard, moreover, was making friends with the county families through the medium of his hound sales – sales which he conducted in person at The Corner. This was a lucrative business, resulting in a daily turnover of anything up to 500 guineas, with the advantage that hacks and hunters were frequently offered at the end of the day. The horses caused the fodder bills to rise, but attracted a wider clientele. There was always a good market for horses of every description.

However, with all his grand schemes, Richard never neglected the smaller clients so necessary to give his transactions a broad base. His detractors said that he would sell his mother's old clothes if he could make a profit. This was certainly not literally true. 'A man should stick to his trade', said Richard, 'and my business is buying and selling horses.' But not every horse, nor at any cost. Richard knew well that if he was to succeed in his profession he must do his best to satisfy buyer and seller alike – an aim unusual among horse-dealers, perhaps, but an ideal on which he founded his business and his reputation. 'Better lose commission than lose a friend', he said, and practised what he preached by letting his customers go elsewhere if he felt he could not satisfy them.

Meanwhile a thoroughbred colt had been born in 1774 that was to have immense significance for the career of Richard Tattersall. By King Herod (also known as Herod) out of Rachel, the foal, to whom the name 'Highflyer' was given,

Highflyer – the horse who helped to found Richard Tattersall's fortunes

was born on Sir Charles Bunbury's estate at Great Barton, 20 miles from Newmarket. Highflyer, who had been given his name because he was foaled in a field where some highflyer walnut trees grew, was sold to Lord Bolingbroke and was never beaten, though some experts claimed years later that he was defeated in a sweepstake run at Newmarket in October 1777. However, James Weatherby, Keeper of the Match Book and Secretary to the Jockey Club, asserted categorically in the first volume of the *General Stud Book* that Highflyer never paid a forfeit, and was never beaten. His racecourse record attracted many covetous eyes but the claim that the famous horse eventually became the property of Richard Tattersall in settlement of a debt owed to him by the profligate Lord Bolingbroke has never been substantiated. The substantiated fact is that the sale was effected on 29 March 1779, the agreed price paid by Tattersall being £2500. Highflyer ran four more times in the name of Richard Tattersall, walking over at Nottingham, winning subscription purses on consecutive days at York and a 100-guineas King's Purse at Lichfield.

A fortnight before Highflyer's victories at York, Richard organized the first Tattersall Sale to be advertised in the press, with notices being placed in both the *Morning Post* and the *Daily Advertiser* that at 12 noon on 11 August carriage horses, ponies, geldings, mares and hacks would be sold. The success of the sale made Richard more determined than ever to settle in London; and the death of his elder brother John during the year, followed by his inheritance and subsequent sale of the Lancashire property of Hurstwood, facilitated his plans.

At the end of his racing career Highflyer was retired to stud near the cathedral city of Ely, where Richard Tattersall had bought the 60-acre Red Barn Farm. Richard's plan was to give Highflyer every chance to take Herod's place as a stallion. Herod's were big shoes to step into and the sire that could wear them would be sought after up and down the land. On the other hand, breeders were still falling over one another in their anxiety to acquire stock bred by the great Eclipse. Eclipse was not for sale – his owner Dennis O'Kelly found him far too profitable for that – and Richard had to consider how his Highflyer would stand in the market against Eclipse and Eclipse's sons.

His solution was brilliant. He would combine the blood of the two by getting every daughter of Eclipse that he could and mating her with Highflyer. 'Send me your Eclipse mares,' he told all his friends, 'and you shall have the best racehorses in England as a result.' Convinced that Highflyer was sent from Heaven as the ideal mate for Eclipse's daughters, he bought a number of them himself and planned to sell them, in foal to Highflyer, at a maximum profit.

Meanwhile, O'Kelly was making hay while the sun shone. In 1781 he won the Derby with Young Eclipse (by Eclipse) and three years later won the race again with another son of Eclipse, Sergeant. Sergeant, as Richard ruefully observed, was out of a Herod mare. It was the right combination of blood but, from Richard's point of view, the wrong way round.

But Highflyer was getting good foals. The mares came to him in a steady stream, never too many for Richard nor, it seemed, for his stalwart stallion. The stud fees came rolling in and, as honest Richard took care to point out, his services were worth every penny of the 15 guineas which he charged for them. The fee was raised to 25 guineas in 1789, to 30 guineas in 1790 and to 50 guineas in 1792.

Highflyer's first sons and daughters appeared on the Turf in 1783, when he had one winner. He had two runners in the Derby of 1784 – Pharamond and Steady – and in the following year his son Verjuice finished third of the ten runners. This minor success was not allowed to be passed over unnoticed, either at Red Barn, where he stood, or in London; Richard's wine merchants noted with satisfaction that his accounts increased steadily.

By 1785 the Hyde Park Corner establishment was beginning to assume considerable proportions. The house and office buildings were modest enough, but the coach houses, kennels and stables occupied a great deal of ground: together with the exercise yards, they covered an area of anything from ten to fifteen acres. Tattersalls was described in Ackermann's *Microcosm of London* as having had accommodation for 120 horses, a large number of carriages, hound kennels and space for harness and all kinds of tackle. Horses, hounds, carriages and the rest came from long distances, and Richard had to find room for them all, plus the attendant grooms, before, during and after the sales.

Hound sales up to 1783 had been conducted under the auspices of 'Mr Tattersall'. By the spring of 1784, however, the auctioneers began to style themselves 'Tattersall and Son'.

The clerks had to work a little harder, too, in order to include the full pedigrees of the hounds on the catalogues – if single or two-page printed bills could be so styled.

The entry to the establishment was through an arched passage and down an inclined drive, at the bottom of which was the Turf Tavern, with its 'tap'. One suspects that it was a glorious 'rough house' on occasion.

On the left, according to an early volume of *Old and New London*, an open gateway led into an enclosure, with a single tree in the centre rising from the middle of a grass plot, surrounded by a circular path of yellow sand or gravel. On the right of the passage a covered gateway led into the courtyard, where the principal business of the place was carried on; this was surrounded on three sides by a covered way, and at the extremity of one side stood the auctioneer's rostrum, overlooking the whole area. The stables, where the horses to be sold were kept in the interim, were close at hand, and admirably arranged for light and ventilation. In the centre of the enclosure was a domed structure housing a pump.

The main building consisted of the offices, a dining room and the two rooms which Richard had placed at the disposal of members of the Jockey Club; these were well served by kitchens and what are known as 'domestic offices'. With these were incorporated, at about this time, the amenities of the original Turf Tavern, which served as an adjunct to the dining room.

Richard went to great pains over the equipment of the dining room. It was, we are told, 'uncommonly elegant and was fitted up at a very great expense; the ceiling alone, which is adorned with allegorical paintings, cost eight hundred guineas'. The Monday dinners, inaugurated in Richard's reign, became an institution. They used to begin sedately enough, but were protracted well into the afternoon and often did not break up until late in the evening. It is on record that Mr John Warde ('glorious John'), M F H and High Sheriff of Kent, prided himself on never missing one of these functions. He had a playful habit of tossing off the contents of a silver fox-head – a matter of a pint of port wine – as a final gesture at the end of the banquet, and then rising, as steady as a rock, to call for his carriage. A model of good manners, he insisted on making his way upstairs to bid farewell to Mrs Tattersall in her drawing room before leaving.

No such premises as Tattersalls could be complete without a Subscription Room – a room which for Tattersall's purpose was a place for the striking and payment of bets. This room was added towards the end of Richard's reign, and subsequently was enlarged to cope with a growing volume of business.

Although Richard himself seldom if ever had a wager, his delight at the success of Noble in the 1786 Derby was boundless, for Noble was a son of Highflyer and the first of his three progeny to win the Epsom Classic. The following year Highflyer's son Sir Peter Teazle won for the young Earl of Derby, and Skyscraper triumphed for the Duke of Bedford in 1789. The success of Highflyer as a stallion persuaded Richard Tattersall to build a country house on the Red Barn Stud estate, to which he proudly gave the name of Highflyer Hall. Once the house was completed Richard proved the perfect host; his cellars were stocked with the finest wines, with which he plied his guests liberally. These guests frequently included the Prince of Wales, Charles James Fox and Charles Wyndham. He became as renowned for his hospitality at Highflyer Hall as he was in London, but he was not oblivious to the financial rewards that such hospitality brought. Equally he genuinely enjoyed acting as host and in his later years told the story that as a young man he had on one occasion invited his creditors to dinner. Each guest found under his plate the sum that Richard owed to him, plus interest.

Meanwhile Highflyer was maintaining his reputation as the best stallion in England. However, all good things have to come to an end, and on 18 October 1793 Richard Tattersall returned from Newmarket to be greeted with the news that his hero and champion was dead.

Highflyer was nineteen years old when he died. He had gained an imperishable reputation as one of the greatest stallions of all time. He was champion sire of winners 12 times, compared with the 8 times of his sire King Herod and the 10 times of his son Sir Peter Teazle. His progeny included the Derby winners Noble, Sir Peter and Skyscraper, the Oaks winner Volante, and the St Leger winners Omphale, Cowslip, Spadille and Young Flora.

Richard had been receiving as much as £2000 a year from Highflyer's stud fees while he was in his prime, but that was small money compared with the commissions he made from the sales of the Highflyer stock, in most of which he had a hand. In addition to his policy of buying all the Eclipse mares he could lay his hands on, and of mating them with Highflyer, he contrived to get the pick of the Highflyer mares into his stud, and, for the best part of eight or nine years, had sold their produce at top prices.

Richard Tattersall did not survive his famous horse for long. By the standards of his times he was a wealthy man. In addition to his profitable enterprises as breeder and auctioneer, he was receiving £1200 a year from a tenant farmer who leased much of his land adjoining Highflyer Hall, and also owned a 1000-acre estate at Littleport Fen. For sentimental reasons he repurchased the Hurstwood property, but it only remained in the Tattersall family for a few years before it was once more sold. He disposed of his interest in the *Morning Post*, which had been an unprofitable venture since he had acquired an interest in 1783, and spent much of his remaining days in retirement at his beloved Highflyer Hall. He died on Saturday 21 February 1795, at his home at Hyde Park. Two days later the *Morning Post* published an obituary;

On Saturday last, at Hyde Park Corner, this worthy and venerable character paid the debt of nature. He died as he lived, as tranquil in his mind as benevolent and humane in his disposition. His loss all must regret who had a knowledge of his worth, and all must severely lament who required his aid and assistance. His greatest delight was in administering to the happiness of mankind; and none who knew his merits there are who will not bear testimony of his friendship as a man, and his feelings as a philanthropist. From his indefatigable industry, and the justice of his dealings, he acquired a degree of affluence which was exercised to the general good, unaccompanied by ostentation, and in his departure from life, he left a lesson to others, that wealth well applied, while it renders existence enviable, affords a consolation in the hour of trial, that every good man must be anxious to emulate and experience.

In another newspaper an epitaph of dubious literary merit was published. It began:

> Here lieth Tattersall, of Turf renown!
> Who, with his hammer, many a Lot knocked down.

Richard, who had appointed James Weatherby as one of his

executors, bequeathed the bulk of his estate to his son, Edmund, who was thirty-seven years old when his father died. Two years earlier Richard Tattersall had commenced the legal process of transferring the control of the family firm to his son, being content in the knowledge that he was a wise administrator dedicated to the aggrandizement of the business.

Edmund Tattersall 1758–1810

At the time of his father's death, Edmund Tattersall was a man of affluence who owned the lease of The Corner and the house in which he lived. Far more cultured than his father as a result of extensive tours on the Continent, his real interest lay not in auctioneering in London or Newmarket, but in hunting. Whenever possible he spent his days with the Royal Buckhounds, yet curiously he had little enthusiasm for the stud at Highflyer Hall, and one of his first acts after his inheritance was to sell the bloodstock, including 34 mares, at The Corner on 1 June 1795, only three months after his father's death.

For the next five years Edmund diligently wooed Lord Grosvenor's agent with regard to leasing land to the west of Hyde Park Corner, but it was no easy task to persuade the Grosvenor estates to allow him to lease the land that he wanted. Ever thoughtful of the future, he took his son Richard into partnership when he attained his majority in 1806, and

Edmund Tattersall (1758–1810). From the painting by Barenger

allowed him to manage the day-to-day administration. The final four years of his life were not unhappy, but soon after Christmas 1809 his doctors diagnosed fever of the brain, and he died on 23 January 1810.

Richard Tattersall ('Old Dick'), 1785–1859

Richard Tattersall spent his youth at Dawley and grew up sharing the family love of hunting, deriving especial pleasure from his runs with Lord Derby's hounds on the Surrey–Hampshire borders. He was twenty-five years old when his father died, and at the time was living at the house at The Corner with his mother and his two brothers, Edmund and George. Within days of his father's death he inserted an advertisement in the *Morning Post*:

> Horses, Carriages, Etc.
>
> Messrs Tattersalls beg leave humbly to solicit of the Nobility, Gentry, and the Public at Large, a continuation of those favours so amply bestowed upon their deceased Father, trusting their conduct in business will be found such as to render them not unworthy of the confidence with which they may be honoured. They continue to sell at Hyde Park Corner, every Monday and Thursday, in the Winter months, and at Newmarket during the Meeting.

Sound common sense caused this insertion, for there were plenty of rivals waiting to profit by any lapse by Tattersalls. Yet provided Richard kept his business acumen the future of his firm was assured. The bloodstock market was not as strong as that for coach and riding horses, but foreign trade continued to be highly profitable, and Richard found himself in the enviable position of being a wealthy young man. In 1811 he sold the bloodstock of the 3rd Duke of Grafton, the second Prime Minister in English history to own a Derby winner, and four years later opened his new Subscription Rooms at The Corner for the settling of debts. He never approved of heavy gambling, preferring the aura of the sale ring, but appreciated that it would be in his best interests to provide Rooms where the betting element of his clientele could congregate. Invariably 'settling' day was Monday and if a classic meeting had been held the previous week settling could take all day. Richard never bet and frequently attempted to dissuade friends from doing so.

In the spring of 1818 a contemporary wrote:

Let us . . . take a general view of the busy scene at Tattersalls, where Peers and other movers in high life descend to be quite men of business, at times – where such a large portion of rank and of fashion is occasionally assembled – and where I was drawn, neither as a dealer nor for a lounge, but merely to meet a friend, who went to purchase a young ruined rake's fine set of carriage horses, and from whom I wanted to get a couple of franks for the Dowager Lady.

A masquerade could scarcely exhibit more motley groups than the attendants of this place of fashionable resort. There were Peers, Baronets, Members of Parliament, Turf-gentlemen and Turf-servants, Jockies, Grooms, Horse-dealers, Gamblers, and Spies. There you might see the oldest and some of the best blood in England, disguised like coachmen, or like the whippers-in of a pack of hounds; there, master and man consulting about the purchase or the sale of a horse; in one place a person of rank taking advice of a horse-jockey or a dealer, on the subject of some match or race; in another, a fat grazier or a flashy butcher, aping the gentleman, in new boots, etc. and come in order to pick up a bargain; one corner displayed the anxious disappointed countenance of a seller; the opposite one discovered the elated, yet perhaps more completely gulled, buyer, who was paying cent per cent for fashion, or half as much again for a pedigreed horse as he was worth, and whose pedigree was, probably, made out only by the horse-dealer. In the centre of the crowd, stood idlers, loungers, gentlemen who had nothing to do but to attend sales without purchasing, and to promenade the parks without knowing or being known to anyone. These were discernible by the apathy of their unmoved features.

By 1820 the influence of Tattersalls was paramount in the world of bloodstock auctioneering, even though other repositories like Aldridges, the Barbican and Sadlers were held in esteem. Tattersall was complimented as 'a more fair-minded man breathes not the air of heaven – the youngest and the most inexperienced may with safety rely on his word, and purchase without hazard'. Perhaps an even greater compliment was paid to him by a notorious highwayman, who stopped him one night when he was in the north of England. After riding alongside in silence for a few hundred yards the highwayman remarked, 'I think your name is Tattersall.' When Richard Tattersall replied in the affirmative his unwanted companion replied, 'I beg your pardon, Sir, I wish you a pleasant end to your journey,' before disappearing into the night.

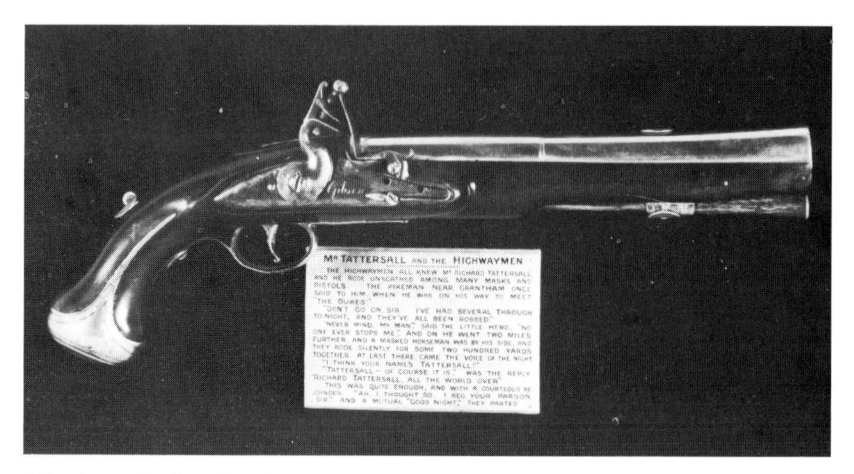

The legend of Richard Tattersall and the highwayman

Occasionally Tattersalls were expected to conduct unusual sales; one such sale was of a collection of young foxes and the skeleton of Eclipse. The sale of the foxes amused Richard's great friend Charles James Apperley (Nimrod) with whom Richard, now dignified as 'Old Dick', and his son, 'Young Richard', visited Germany in 1828 as the guests of Baron Biel. The party were lavishly entertained during the trip, and 'Old Dick' competed in a steeplechase, finishing second. He enjoyed the race, but his happiest moments still came when he was either hunting – particularly stag-hunting with Lord Derby's hounds from The Oaks, or driving the Peterborough coach, for he was a first-class whip.

Lame since boyhood as a result of a groom giving him a rough leg-up onto a pony, Richard found his injured knee some hardship in middle age, causing him to choose a hard-pulling horse whenever possible. In his youth he had been a fine boxer and it was claimed that he would have been champion of England if he had not been lame.

Trade with the Continent steadily increased, with a continual stream of orders from Germany, France, Austria, Russia and Holland. One of the most regular buyers was a German, Mr Lichtwald. At Goodwood in 1839 his colt, Hyllis, finished second to Harkaway – the one horse that everyone wished to buy. Richard Tattersall even had a commission from America to buy him, but his Irish owner refused to sell, stating categorically, 'the price of Harkaway is 6000 guineas and I hunt him twice a week'.

Sales at Doncaster, Hampton Court and The Corner also flourished; the decision of some of the major studs to sell their yearlings annually meant that this became one of Tattersall's chief sources of business. One momentous sale occurred on 25 October 1837, when Richard Tattersall conducted the sale at Hampton Court Paddocks, where the Royal Stud was broken up shortly after the accession of the young Queen Victoria. The majority of the 81 lots sold badly, but the stallions fared better, and The Colonel, hero of the 1828 St Leger, was bought by 'Old Dick' for 1550 guineas and sent to his stud farm at Dawley. Significantly, a subtle change was beginning to affect the relationship between Tattersalls and those who bought and sold horses from them. During past decades these men had been patrons: now they were acknowledged as clients and customers, with The Corner adapting itself to the new needs.

Richard was forever being pressed to sell his horses under

Richard Tattersall (1785–1859) at the rostrum

warranty, but he refused to accede to these requests. He said to his staff:

> You can tell the customers that every horse that comes to the Yard for the Monday Sales is there from four o'clock on the previous Friday afternoon. They can see them as much as they like; they can try them in the exercising yard if they want to. Beyond that I will not go.

There was some very good common sense in this arrangement, which, incidentally, had been the firm's policy from the start. The buyer had to take the risk. At least at Tattersalls the goods were there for the customer to inspect. In practice, groom could talk to groom, and the master could make his bid on the strength of his own judgement, supported by the information which it was his servant's business to provide.

In 1840 'Old Dick' and his younger brother, Edmund, took 'Young Richard', son of 'Old Dick', into partnership. Born in 1812, he had travelled extensively in Europe and the United States of America as a young man. By the time he became a partner he was fully conversant with every aspect of the business and, more significantly, other members of the family had complete confidence in his ability.

Three years later 'Old Dick' published new rules and regulations concerning the Subscription Rooms at The Corner. The Jockey Club were attempting to divorce themselves from the responsibility of settling betting disputes, and were in full agreement on the subject with 'Old Dick', who

The scene at Tattersalls at 'The Corner', circa 1840

abhorred gambling, even though he realized the importance of maintaining his Rooms. He was a deeply religious man, rigorously opposed to any kind of chicanery. Nothing made him more angry than a suggestion that a dealers' ring was operating at his sales.

In 1844 'Old Dick' Tattersall gave evidence before the Special Committee on the Gaming Laws, presided over by Lord Palmerston. It was a long interview, spread over several days during the spring. He agreed that persons engaged in betting upon horse-races were in the habit of meeting at The Corner and that they paid an annual subscription of two guineas. For this subscription members could enter the Rooms every Monday and Thursday, and also on the Thursday following the Derby. In the course of his evidence 'Old Dick' Tattersall was asked if he was of the opinion that it would be desirable to legalize betting and bets, and to make bets recoverable in a court of law. He replied:

I am sure it would prevent an amazing deal of betting, and it would prevent a great many people being ruined, because there are a great many men that go for a stake that never mean to pay if they lose.

He was then asked:

You say that it would be desirable to legalize betting, and to give the power of recovering a bet by a legal remedy in a court of justice?

He replied:

Yes; you cannot now seize a person for a common debt as you used to do. A man would come to my house and buy horses and then laugh at me if I trusted him; formerly I could arrest those persons, now I cannot, and they laugh at me; and it is the same with betting; they bet with a man and lose a good deal of money to him; they say, 'I cannot afford to pay you just now, you must give me time;' and they go again and lose and laugh at the man, and you cannot recover it by any means, but if you could by law you would have a resource. There are many men now that live by betting. I heard a man say myself, after he had lost a great deal of money, when he was called upon to pay his debts (he had lost a great deal of money upon the turf), he said: 'Do you suppose I am going to ruin myself for those blackguards; what am I to do for my family?'

Later in the interview he gave his opinion upon the relative value of horses. He was questioned as follows.

Q. You are a very large breeder of horses without running them and you have also been employed to sell very large studs in this country, and to purchase them for foreigners, and you know the relative value of horses in this country and other countries?'
A. Yes.
Q. Will you state what you consider creates the value of a thoroughbred horse in this country?
A. The engagements he is entered for as a foal, and the more engaged, the more valuable.
Q. And the possibility there is of winning large sums of money by him?
A. Yes.
Q. But for that system, do you think the foreign governments would come and purchase our best horses?
A. Yes; it is from that impression of horses having run and distinguished themselves in this way, that they sell at such immense sums.
Mr V. Smith Are foreigners often buyers of horses that have distinguished themselves?
A. Yes, Priam was sold at one year old for 1000 guineas; he was purchased in consequence of his being in some of the largest engagements. His forfeits, supposing he had not started for any one of those races, were £450. The horse went on, and Lord Chesterfield soon after he had come out asked me to advise him to buy a horse; I advised him to buy Priam. After Priam ran his first race I bid Chifney 5000 guineas for that horse, because he was so well engaged. In that year he won £9500 public money. I wrote a cheque for 5000 guineas: the man was a trainer, but he was so confident that he would win his engagements that he refused the 5000 guineas. I afterwards gave £3000 for that horse for Lord Chesterfield, and I gave £3700 for him to Lord Chesterfield to go to America; my order then was unlimited.
Colonel Peel Nothing but the large stakes they run for in America at those times enabled them to give that money?
A. Of course not.
Q. If racing was discouraged and the stakes reduced in this country, the breed of horses would decline?
A. Of course, I breed largely; if I have 20 foals and 10 of those foals are in the Derby and other great stakes, they are worth 300 or 400 guineas apiece to me, but if they were not in those stakes they would not be worth above 120.
Mr V. Smith Do not you hear from the dealers in all parts of the

kingdom that the great purchasers are foreigners?
A. At a certain price.
Q. At a high price?
A. No; our people will give higher prices.
Colonel Peel The greater the demand in this country, whether for foreigners or for our own people, the greater the encouragement to breeders?
A. Yes, certainly.
Q. The French Government purchase horses to breed from?
A. Yes, they do.
Q. Which in this country is all done by private individuals?
A. Yes, Government do it in France; they have 150 stallions, all kept by the Government, and they cover for nothing, for a guinea or something of that sort; whereas we keep our horses, and pay for them ourselves. I sold a horse for £1000 the other day.
Q. You have been in the habit of attending at Doncaster races?
A. Yes.
Q. Do not you think that there was a great deal more betting upon the Doncaster St Leger than there is now?
A. The betting has been going off for years as to large sums of money.
Mr Cochrane How do you account for that?
A. There are not so many gentlemen who keep horses, and there are not so many people that have money to bet.
Mr Escott Are people poorer than they used to be?
A. We horse people are. The hunters do not fetch half the price that they used to do.
Q. Is not the general price of horses in this country as high as it used to be?
A. No.
Colonel Peel Is that caused by the railways?
A. Entirely.
Chairman You have had an opportunity of observing the character of the breed of horses generally, in this country; do you think that within the last 20 or 25 years the breed of horses in general has improved or not?
A. I think that the breed of horses is improved; but there are not so many bred.
Mr Cochrane Do you think that if betting were put an end to entirely, it would diminish racing and put down the breeding of horses?
A. If betting were put an end to there would be an end of my breeding; I cannot bring a horse up to be a yearling under £120.

The Commission were also interested in the expense involved in keeping horses in training, and questioned him on this score

Q. Can you state to the Committee the annual Expense of keeping Ten Brood Mares?

A. The Expense of keeping Brood Mares depends on various Causes. If you have a good Stallion at home you save travelling Expenses, Men Etc., Etc. The great Expense is building loose Boxes, Yards, Etc., which must be added to the Keep, as it is for them they are built. Ten mares require the constant Attendance of Two Men, well fed, plenty of Corn, Etc., I should say, as Corn and Hay now is, every Mare costs £40 per Annum, without the Price of Covering.

Q. Can you state the Expense of keeping ten Brood Mares and Foals?

A. The Expense of Ten Brood Mares and Foals, until weaning Time, with plenty of Corn, Bran, Carrots, Etc., the Foals cost 5s per week.

Q. Can you state to the Committee the Expense incurred after a Foal is weaned until it is of proper Age to be sent to the Trainers to be broke and trained?

A. The Expense of keeping a Foal until broke would be about 15s. per Week; breaking £5 extra.

Q. What is the usual Charge of a Trainer per Week for each Horse?

A. Two guineas per Week, and shoeing, Etc., Etc., not included.

Q. Has not the Practice of sending Race Horses in Vans much increased the Expense to Race Horse Owners?

A. Greatly, as they are obliged to post with Four Horses, and pay very high on the Rail.

Q. Are not many Horses put out of training every Year, and sold, not having been found good enough to continue in training?

A. I sell a great many Horses every Year that are put out of training, and found not good enough to keep on at the great Expense, and some are turned into Hacks, Etc., Etc.

Q. Would a Race Horse Owner, without a very great Sacrifice of Money, be enabled to continue on the Turf if his Horse would only win £100 on each Race?

A. No man could keep Race Horses if small Stakes were run for. No Man keeps a Race Horse for less than £230, besides Jockey for riding.

Q. How would he do on small Stakes, as £100?

A. He might be entered for Six or Eight Races, pay Forfeit for Four or Six, and thus win £200. This would very soon destroy the Breed of Horses in England, which now brings Thousands from all Parts of the World.

Richard Tattersall (1785–1859). From an engraving

The year 1844 also found Richard Tattersall on the fringe of the 'Running Rein' scandal, which rocked racing England. His involvement reached its zenith on settling day at The Corner on the Monday after the Derby had been contested. Few other than Lord George Bentinck and the perpetrators of the crime, headed by Levi Goodman, whom Bentinck was attempting to bring to justice, knew the true facts, but there were a considerable number of men who thought that they might be able to avoid payment of their debts. Colonel Peel (afterwards General), the owner of Orlando who had finished second, had immediately claimed the stake, no doubt persuaded to do so by Bentinck, who was determined that Goodman should not be allowed to make fools of the Jockey Club. Admiral Rous also was aware of the facts, while John Bowes wrote to his solicitor: 'Running Rein belongs to a party of vagabonds who were at the bottom of Mr Russell's "Qui Tam" actions – they have won largely but I hope that we shall be able to prove the horse four years old as he undoubtedly is . . .'

Throughout the Saturday and the Sunday following the Derby the only topic of conversation at Tattersalls was the Running Rein scandal, but sensibly the Tattersalls Committee posted an instruction on the Monday morning:

At a meeting of the most influential subscribers to Tattersalls interested in the Derby and Oaks settlement, it was unanimously agreed that no possible impediment could exist to the settlement of all accounts on the Derby in which the names of Running Rein and Orlando do not occur, and that, therefore, the settling will take place this day as usual with the above exceptions.

The reference to the Oaks concerned the filly Julia, to whom Colonel Anson and Squire Osbaldeston lodged an objection before the race on the grounds that she was not the filly described in the nomination. Julia was allowed to run but was unplaced.

Another complication concerning the Derby settlement was the death of William Crockford on Saturday 25 May, three days after the Derby. Crockford died a rich man, but nevertheless there were those at Tattersalls who claimed that, by precedent, his death absolved the settlement of debts due to him. They were silenced when, two days after his death, his widow sent a letter to Richard Tattersall:

Sir – I trust the circumstances which cause me to address you will be a sufficient apology for so doing. Being ignorant of the custom in use at Tattersalls in situations parallel to the one I now find myself placed in, I consider it best for me at once to place in your hands the betting books of my deceased husband. You will perceive that in case Running Rein shall receive the stakes, there will be a loss of £604, and in case Orlando shall receive them, a loss of £724. I enclose you therefore a draft for the larger sum, and would wish you to apply this sum, together with the receipts from the several losers, to pay as far as may be the claims of the several winners. It is possible that, in a case of this sort, it is not customary to settle the book. Should it be so, I am not anxious to establish a precedent. With a deep sense of the trouble I am about to impose upon you, I have the honour to be, sir, yours most respectfully,

S.F. Crockford.
Carlton House Terrace, May 27 1844.

'Old Dick' Tattersall also received a letter from the Stewards of the Jockey Club, signed by the Earl of Stradbroke and the Hon. George Byng, that every person indebted to the late Mr Crockford on his Epsom account was bound to pay the amount due to the person deputed to settle the same. Notwithstanding the honesty of Mrs Crockford, there were several who refused to settle their Derby and Oaks commitments.

In July, when the lawsuit was over, and the Derby awarded to Orlando, *The Times* fired a broadside:

> It was well known long ago that they would be 'wanted' if Orlando won and no one is in the least surprised at their absence. These deficiences and the state of abeyance in which the late Mr Crockford's book remains, has a most disheartening influence on the settlement, all the accounts having been more or less disarranged, and several parties, good winners on the race, obliged in consequence to leave the Room considerably out of pocket. The only way to prevent this very unusual consequence of extravagant and indiscriminate 'Bookmaking' is without regard to rank or station, to adopt the 'blackboard', and post not only actual defaulters, but all who fail to attend or make arrangements for paying and receiving on the regular settling day.

Four years later, after Lord George Bentinck had sold his horses to Lord Mostyn, it was proposed that a mammoth bloodstock sale be conducted by Tattersalls at Goodwood – but the idea came to naught as the Duke of Richmond raised objections. Instead, 'Old Dick' sold a draft of nineteen broodmares, three yearlings and eight horses in training at Tattersalls. In aggregate the thirty lots fetched £3720.

In December 1851 Edmund, the younger brother of 'Old Dick', died at the age of sixty-two. He was very short-sighted and never played a prominent part in the family business, although he had been a partner for almost forty years. 'Old Dick' was now sixty-six years old, and inevitably the death of his younger brother made him conscious that he should take steps towards preparing for his own retirement. It was a sensible decision, for his health was deteriorating, and his wife was anxious that he should take life more easily. He was complaining of headaches and drowsiness and increasingly requested his son to take a more active part in the business.

Edmund Tattersall (1789–1851). From the painting by Hurlstan

In the North his greatest friend was Sir Tatton Sykes of Sledmere, a man of the most lovable disposition and one who was acknowledged to exemplify the perfect English gentleman and sportsman. When Sykes was seventy years old he attended the theatre in Doncaster with Richard Tattersall. They were sitting in the back row of the boxes when a large blustering man came in with a cigar in his mouth. As there were ladies in the box he was asked to put it out. The man refused, with the result that Richard Tattersall, always a strong and powerful man despite his lameness, opened the door with one hand and threw out the objectionable intruder with the other. He stormed and blustered, but to no avail as Richard, deaf to his threats of revenge, returned to his seat. On another occasion Sir Tatton Sykes had bid 3000 guineas for Fandango, but was so anxious to buy the horse that he bid another 100 guineas. When Richard Tattersall diplomatically reminded him from the rostrum that the previous bid was also his, he pulled out his watch and said 'Knock him down, Mr Tattersall, knock him down. We want to go to the races.'

Richard continued to preside at dinners and discussed

current racing affairs with his countless friends at The Corner. Above all else, however, his mind was occupied by the fact that the Grosvenor Estates would not renew the lease upon The Corner.

The Corner had developed considerably since Richard first went there as a young man in 1810. Its rural aspect had survived, but the lawn in front of the main entrance had been mown; and gravel paths replaced the rough alleyways leading to the Yards. The public had been excluded from the Yard's precincts by means of that remarkable product of the Victorian era, the iron railing; the offices and stable accommodation had been enlarged. The entrance was through a small lane or passage leading from Grosvenor Place. St George's Hospital occupied the corner, as now; to the south was Grosvenor Crescent, to the south-west, Belgrave Square. The ground ran westward towards Wilton Crescent; the Barracks were to the north-west, and the newly built Alexandra Hotel, and the houses between it and the hospital, formed the northern boundary.

The building itself was on the left of the little lane, and was entered through the same old arched passage, leading to the inclined drive, at the bottom of which was the old Turf Tavern, converted in Richard's day to the Subscription Rooms. Beyond this was the Courtyard, with its pump; further away still were the stabling and kennels. The Five Fields, to the west and south-west, were no more. The Victorians were building Belgravia, as only they knew how. The Courtyard, open to the sky, had as its principal architectural feature the pump, with its fox and its dome.

In *Post and Paddock* The Druid gave a personal impression of Tattersalls' Subscription Rooms during this era:

The room which bears silent witness to these ceaseless flirtations with the goddess Fortune, is 45 by 28 feet, and capable of holding about 400 persons. In the middle of it is a sort of circular counter, round which and the fireplace the business is principally transacted; but in the summer the room is nearly deserted, and speculation adjourns on to the steps and green outside, and holds communication with its less favoured votaries through the iron bars of the gate.

Although the numbers fluctuate considerably, the Room has about as many subscribers as it can hold; a great increase on the number who adjourned there in Attila's year, from their small trysting-place lower down the lane. Candidates are elected by the committee of the Room; they must find a nominator and a seconder, and the names must be up for at least a month.

The left side windows open out on to the terrace green, where the Ring, weather permitting, stand or saunter about on field days; and masters of hounds, etc., earlier in the morning try the paces of a hack they may have been eyeing in some of the 120 stalls in the adjacent yard; but on off days it is more associated in our minds with a walnut-tree, and an Alderney cow, and a pail. Such are the leading features of the great betting mart, whose quotations are to racing men what those of Mark Lane are to the farmer, Lloyd's to the insurer, the Stock Exchange to the broker, or Greenwich Time to the horologist.

By the beginning of 1859 it was evident that 'Old Dick' was a sick man. A holiday at Dover failed to restore his health, and he died on 22 July 1859. In his will he bequeathed

to my son Richard the gold snuff box given to me by the Duke de Guiche the picture of my grandfather now over the chimney piece of my dining room if he should prefer it to the portrait of the same person now in his possession and should give the latter to my nephew Edmund Tattersall the picture of my father on his horse Hammer the picture of 'Myself on Buonaparte' the Doncaster racing cup and the fox's head I give to my daughter Eliza . . . the album of prints the Duke of Holstein's vase and the picture of her mother by Collin I give to my daughter Mary Charlotte the album of 1820 the glass barrel and the Christening bowl I give to my son-in-law William Courtney Esquire the picture of a cart and horse by Marshall. . . .

In the decade before his death, his son 'Young Richard' and his nephew Edmund, son of farmer and auctioneer George Tattersall, had occasionally discussed the future of the business. Edmund had been a partner since 1851 and his views were sought, especially when Tattersalls' solicitors continued to warn them that the lease on The Corner was due to expire shortly and that the Marquess of Westminster was not prepared to grant them a renewal. The acquisition of alternative premises, therefore, became of paramount importance. These were eventually found at a site near the Albert Gate in Knightsbridge, with the final session at The Corner being held on 8 April 1865.

Five years earlier 'Young Richard' had conducted the Londesborough dispersal sale at Grimston Park near Tadcaster. Amongst the lots were two great horses, Stockwell and West Australian. The sight of two St Leger winners in the sale ring on the same day was not one to be missed; the paddock in which the sale was held was crowded. One old Yorkshireman was completely confounded. 'It beats me', he said. 'These gentlemen, they get fuller of money the longer the day goes on.' At the time, West Australian was more highly esteemed than the other and, when Stockwell was knocked down to the bid of Mr R. C. Naylor at 4500 guineas, it was expected that 'Westy' would realize much more. Unhappily there was no one willing to outbid the Frenchman, Count Morny, who secured him for 4000 guineas, and there were murmurs of vexation and disappointment when he was led out of the ring. Tattersalls, however, had nothing to complain of. The total for the afternoon was 20,689 guineas.

Within six years of the death of 'Old Dick' the Rubicon had been crossed, and the Tattersall cousins had moved the business to its new site. Articles appeared in magazines and newspapers praising the Tattersall family, but bemoaning the loss of 'Old Corner', one of the historic landmarks of London. In his autobiography Lord Brampton tells that:

Tattersalls, in my time, was one of the pleasantest Sunday afternoon lounges in London. There was a spirit of freedom and social equality pervading the place which only belongs to assemblies where sport is the principal object or pleasure of all.

The institution has perhaps known more great men than Parliament itself – not so many bishops, perhaps, as the Church, but more statesmen than could get into the House of Lords.

Here the great and small mingled on terms of friendly intimacy and equality . . . the wit met the fool . . . the rich met the poor. . . . Country squires and Cockney sportsmen talked of the merits of the Flying Dutchman or Voltigeur, Surplice or the losing favourite in the famous Hermit's year.

The names of all the great and mediocre people who visited the famous rendezvous would fill a respectable Court guide, and the money transactions that have taken place would pay off the National Debt . . . illustrious Queen's Counsel . . . authors, editors, actors, statesmen. . . .

At first my visits were infrequent; afterwards I went more often, and then became a regular attendant. I loved the 'Old Ring', and yet could never explain why. . . . There were three principal places of pleasure at that time: one was Tattersall's, one Newmarket, and the Courts of Law a third.

The move to the Albert Gate premises was effected on 10 April 1865, and was celebrated by a testimonial dinner at Willis's Rooms on the following day. The chief signatory to the invitation was Admiral Rous, who took the chair. The party was a private function, and was limited to 300 persons – members of the Jockey Club and the Subscription Rooms and friends of Richard and his associates. A writer in *All the Year Round* gave an eye-witness account of the banquet in the following terms:

The opening of this elegant room was celebrated by the members with a dinner to the Messrs Tattersall, to express the gratitude of the sporting world for its fine new lodgings. I remember me well of that famous banquet; of the hundreds of massive race cups lent by their owners to grace the dinner-table; of the mighty pyramids of flowers, set between the great gold and silver groups and cases, to lighten the general effect; of the asparagus and early strawberries; of the chairman and his hearty manner; of Mr George Payne's witty oration in proposing the health of 'The Ring'; and of the reply thereto by bluff 'Stevey', soon to come to a sad end, poor fellow. I remember me also of . . . my neighbour, who hinted that the gathering offered a fine chance for a modern Guy Fawkes. . . .

The toast of the evening was proposed by Admiral Rous: 'Prosperity to the House of Tattersalls'. He commented that the guests had been invited not to mourn the Old Corner but to congratulate Tattersalls upon the completion of a magnificent building which might be regarded as a national institution. In his reply Richard Tattersall pointed out:

It is now a hundred years, bar one [*much laughter*], since our great-grandfather leased from the Earl Grosvenor the piece of ground on which he established our place of business. He was best known to his contemporaries by the name of 'Old Tatt', and by his honesty and uprightness he acquired the goodwill and respect of all who knew him. The Prince of Wales, afterwards George the Fourth, then a young man, was a constant patron of the establishment. . . . The Prince was also a frequent visitor to my great-grandfather's seat, Highflyer Hall and many strange stories have been told of the Prince and his companions there. Among other things, I have heard of a postchaise galloping into the town of Newmarket at night, with his Royal Highness riding the leaders, and Charles Fox the wheelers. Towards the end of the last century, my great-grandfather was succeeded by his son, my grandfather, who, like his father, had the reputation of being an honourable and an honest man. He was joint proprietor, with the Prince, of the *Morning Post* newspaper. In 1810 my father and uncle succeeded to the business, which they carried on successfully for fifty years. No man, perhaps, was more popular with all classes than my lamented father; and no man, perhaps, ever made more sincere friends, and among others I may mention the name of an English nobleman who was a model in every relation of life – I mean the late Duke of Richmond. Time and the Marquess of Westminster have driven us out of our time-honoured locality, and we have taken a piece of ground as near as we could get it to the Corner. But although we have changed our premises we have not changed our principles, and we hope and trust we may still be honoured with the same confidence and patronage which we have enjoyed for so many years. There is one important point in our establishment upon which I should like to say a few words. Although large sums of money depend upon horse-racing, yet the occupation of the book-maker was a few years since a very small business. It was confined to but few persons. Like the electric telegraph and the railways, it has sprung into importance only of late years, and has now passed from noblemen and gentlemen of high standing and means to persons of lower rank, who, years since, would as soon have thought of keeping a tame elephant as a book. The art of book-making has, however, increased with the number of trainers and horses. In 1818, my father opened a small room, then used as a laundry, in his house for a subscription-room. The number of members gradually increased, until, in 1842, the room not being large enough, a more spacious one for this class of patrons of the establishment was opened on the lawn. That was the room in which we have seen so many ups and downs in horses and races, and where such large sums of money have changed hands during the last few years. That room, however, had also become too small; and in our new premises we have spared no money to make the new room worthy of the objects for which it has been expected; for this portion of the business has now become one of the institutions of the time. In conclusion, I thank you for the handsome manner in which you have spoken of our firm, and for your kind attendance this evening; and as long as I live I shall ever look back to this day as one of the proudest in my existence.

His words were well received, but few of the guests knew that his health was on the wane. The last four years of his life were painful, with pains in his heart and swellings in his legs. He died on 3 May 1870 at the age of fifty-eight. He had lived a full, happy and active life in which he helped many of the country's leading owners and bloodstock breeders to purchase and sell their horses. He introduced the American Ten Broeck to racing England; and was the personal friend of William I'Anson, James Merry and Sir Joseph Hawley. At heart he was a countryman even though he had the wisdom to adapt himself to London society. He and his wife had no children, and when his will was proved, Elizabeth was named as his sole heir and executrix. The death of 'Young Richard' resulted in his cousin Edmund taking control of the business.

Edmund Tattersall, 1816–98

Edmund Tattersall was born on 9 February 1816, less than a year after the battle of Waterloo. He was the elder son of George Tattersall, who never had any connection with the family firm, and his wife Eliza Reeve, whose father was acknowledged to be one of the best tenant farmers on the Holkham estate. At the time of his son's birth George Tattersall was renting a farm near Sculthorpe in Norfolk from Sir Jacob Astley, later Lord Hastings. George encouraged his son to ride before he was seven years old, and days were spent hunting with the Norfolk, Suffolk and East Essex. During the Napoleonic Wars the price of wheat had been high, and consequently George Tattersall had made a comfortable living, but eventually the bubble burst and prices plummeted. Faced with possible ruin George decided to go to London to discuss his situation with his brother Dick, who was affluent and wise. After considerable thought 'Old Dick' decided that auctioneering was not the correct profession for Edmund and suggested that George should take over the family stud farm at Dawley, 3 miles on the London side of Uxbridge.

The farm had been acquired in Old Tatt's day and, if it had not made its name as a first-class breeding establishment, it had served a useful purpose, accommodating broodmares and young stock and also being used as a boarding establishment for the miscellaneous animals which, from time to time, had become the temporary responsibility of the firm. Edmund and George walked the farm and inspected the house, barns, boxes and farm implements. Next morning George drove back to Sculthorpe and told Eliza his news. It was not long before they made up their minds to accept Dick's offer.

George's tenancy and management of the Dawley farm lasted until the late 1830s. The stallions that stood there included Sir Hercules, Glencoe, Charles XII, Harkaway and Recovery.

Edmund Tattersall (1816–1898) on Black Bess. From the painting by Byron Webb

Once the move to Dawley had been made 'Young Edmund' was sent to new Grammar Schools, firstly in Henley, and later in Guildford, but he was at his happiest during the school holidays, when he was a frequent follower of the Queen's Hounds, with which Charles Davis was carrying the horn. Eventually the Great Western Railway was built through the property at Dawley, and there was no option for George Tattersall but to move the bloodstock to another Tattersall farm at Willesden.

The impressionable years spent with the Royal Buckhounds as a young man stood Edmund in good stead in his future career and he became a capital judge of hunters. In the mid-1830s he went into business on his own account as an auctioneer at Newmarket, but in 1851 was persuaded to go to The Corner to assist his uncle, 'Old Dick'. A man with many of the Tattersall characteristics including charm, wit, good taste, and a most persuasive voice, he married Emily Elizabeth Byers on 3 September 1862. During the next few years Edmund Tattersall spent much of his energy in supervising the building of the new premises which were to take the place of the Old Corner on the expiry of the lease. The property occupied a site of almost two acres, and was situated at the eastern apex of the Brompton Road and Knightsbridge Road.

Tattersalls, severe in its walls of grey London brick but planned to accommodate both staff and visitors in comfort, was designed by Charles Freeman and built by Messrs Holland. The architect, having conformed to his client's wishes to provide a sober and suitable façade to the establishment, endowed it with an imposing archway and concentrated his talent for decoration on the adornment of the Subscription Rooms on the left, or southern, side and on a small room in the right-hand building which, for a time, was placed at the disposal of members of the Jockey Club.

The Subscription Room, sixty feet long and thirty feet wide, was extremely handsome, lofty and nobly proportioned. It was lighted from above by three great domes. Its mantels were of marble, its floor of tessellated stone, laid in symmetrical fashion. The panels on the walls were painted in green and gold; on the mantel above the principal fireplace was the Louis Quinze clock which had once graced the old Subscription Room at The Corner. The original furniture

The Tattersalls yard at Knightsbridge

consisted mainly of long seats, upholstered in green morocco leather, placed along the walls; two long mahogany tables faced them, on either side of the length of the room. On one of the walls hung the large oblong painting by Joy, depicting a scene on the lawn of the old Rooms at The Corner.

Many descriptions of the new premises were published, with *Baily's Magazine* explaining in October 1870:

But there is a movement in the crowd at the gate, and Mr Edmund Tattersall, accompanied by Mr Christopher (who is made for riding) walks towards the rostrum, and we see that the real business of the day is about to commence. After a slight pause, followed by one of those speeches with which Mr Tattersall knows so well how to get on terms with his audience, short, sharp, and decisive – of a style, in fact, that the clergy would do well to imitate – the first thoroughbred, the property of Baron Stickler, is brought up; but as yet buyers are not warmed to their work, and he, like several others, is doomed to go at 'hack prices'.

Meanwhile, those who intend business are drawing round as near as the gapers and loungers will allow, while a few favoured ones are admitted into the pulpit itself, amongst whom the stalwart form of

The auctioneer's rostrum at Tattersalls, Knightsbridge

the Admiral is conspicuous, and Mr Blenkiron occupies his usual post when anything good is to be disposed of.

In the archway, examining a horse with such minuteness, is a veterinary from Mount Street, who earns more in one morning by his examinations than half the junior bar of England do at Quarter Sessions. Then passes a jolly comely-looking man who rides a good-shaped brown horse in the Row, and whom we have often seen charging at the head of a troop at the battle of Brighton Downs.

There had been a short period after the move when Tattersalls, as a place for the making and settling of bets, lost some of its custom. The practice among racehorse owners of employing commission agents to do their business had increased and many transactions were carried on elsewhere. The strict enforcement of the various Acts against ready-money betting had forced many of these commission agents to do their business abroad. Some opened offices in Brussels and Paris and, for a while, Tattersall's business suffered accordingly. At no time, however, did the House lose its cachet as a rendezvous for the upper-class sporting world. Mondays at Knightsbridge had their regular place in the engagements of the sporting nobility and gentry.

In March 1866, Edmund had bought Coleherne Court, once the home of Cromwell's generals, whose garden walls and boundaries fronted the Old Brompton Road at its intersection with Earl's Court Road.

The large garden, with its borders and double tennis lawns, was severed from 'the obtrusive ugliness of Redcliffe Square' on the south by a thick belt of oaks, elms, acacias and planes. The entrance to the house was through a covered way.

The hall, whose stone floor was squared with marble edges, had a moulded plaster ceiling in a pattern which was repeated in the principal living-rooms. Edmund and his predecessors had gathered together an almost unique collection of horse portraits, a great number of which were by the master painters of the eighteenth and nineteenth centuries.

On one of the walls of the hall hung a picture of the dead heat between Charles XII and Euclid in the St Leger of 1839. Over the massive lintel of the two inner doors was a picture of Mendicant. Here, too, was a companion portrait of Pyrrhus the First, the pair commemorating the triumphs of the Oaks and Derby winners of 1846; the paintings had at one time been the treasured possessions of Sam Day, who rode them both.

Edmund's own room was a treasure house of pictures,

notable among which were portraits of General Peel, of Lord Jersey's 1825 winner Middleton, and of other famous horses including Harkaway. In the gallery at the head of the stairs were portraits of Sir Henry Hawkins and Sir Evelyn Wood. There was a bust of Lord George Bentinck and statuettes of Warrior and Knight of St Patrick. There were engravings and photographs, cups, trophies, hunting horns, hooves of great horses, whips, spurs and pistols. In the dining room there hung, over a marble mantel brought from The Corner, Carter's painting of Edmund himself, head of the family. On another wall was Zoffany's painting of the old Yard, flanked by a fine portrait of Highflyer and Beach's striking portrait of Old Tatt.

At the end of the 1860s Tattersalls continued to flourish, with a considerable annual trade in hunters and hounds. Edmund Tattersall found himself overworked and took the unprecedented step of taking a man into partnership who was not a member of the family. This was Thomas Pain, a former

Edmund Tattersall (1816–1898). From the painting by S. Carter

Master of the South Wilts who had built up a clientele in the shires, fostering the hunter sales at Rugby and hound sales in the area of Melton Mowbray. Edmund Tattersall never became enthusiastic over the Rugby sales and seldom visited the Midlands, but Pain broadened the base of the firm's operations and filled the gap left by the death of Richard Tattersall.

In the previous year a change had been made at Doncaster, where Tattersalls had conducted their sales outside the Salutation Inn. After the death of Lord Glasgow a lease on the Glasgow Paddocks, which adjoined the racecourse, was taken. Yet trade there was limited at that period compared with the annual turnover at Newmarket, and the studs at Hampton Court, Cobham and Middle Park. The Royal Stud at Hampton Court resumed operation in 1851, with annual sales of yearlings. In 1888 a colt by Springfield was sold there for 5000 guineas and two years later won the Derby under the name of Sainfoin.

Not content with the furtherance of his plans for the Doncaster Sales, Edmund had turned his attention in 1870 to the improvement of the Newmarket organization. The July Sales had hitherto been conducted on a piece of land behind Queensberry House, not far from the Jockey Club premises in the High Street. Edmund, however, had long had his eye on a few nearby fields which adjoined the McCalmont estate. He negotiated for the hiring of a part of them, and for a spell of fourteen years the sales were conducted there in the open air. The field in which the horses were assembled sloped down towards what is now known as 'the Avenue', which leads from the High Street to the railway station. There was neither a ring nor a stand; a few carriages and wagons were its only 'props'.

The site was an improvement on the old ground, but it was realized at the time that it would need to be extended. The death in 1884 of the owner of the land, Sir Richard Wallace, provided the opportunity for expansion which Edmund had long desired. Negotiations were started with the executors in due course and, before the year was out, Tattersalls had bought it outright. Architects and builders were consulted and, in a very short time, the new premises were built. The ring, the seating around it, the rostrum, offices, and the little refreshment room – the use of which, until about 1940, was reserved for the firm's privileged guests – were added in due course, and boxes constructed for the accommodation of the horses.

The year 1872 saw Edmund Tattersall conduct the mammoth four-day dispersal sale at the Middle Park Stud at Eltham in Kent, which had been established by William Blenkiron as one of the first commercial breeding operations. Tattersalls had conducted the annual Middle Park yearling sales, which had produced such top-class horses as the Derby winners Caractacus and Hermit. The dispersal sale realized the gigantic total of 107,000 guineas. The climax was reached on the final day when the eleven-year-old stallion Blair Athol, winner of the Derby and St Leger, was brought into the ring. Edmund demanded, 'Now, gentlemen, what may I say for the best horse in the world?' Minutes later the great horse was acquired by the Cobham Stud Company for 12,500 guineas.

Twelve years later, in January 1884, Edmund conducted another great dispersal sale when Lord Falmouth, then at the zenith of his fame as an owner-breeder, commissioned him to sell all his horses in training and breeding stock. This choice

Hermit, the winner of the 'snowstorm Derby', 1867. Purchased by Mr Henry Chaplin for 1000 guineas as a yearling at the Middle Park Sales, conducted by Tattersalls. From the painting by Ben Herring

St Simon, one of the greatest racehorses and stallions of all time, cast in bronze by Sir Edgar Boehme. Purchased by the Duke of Portland for 1600 guineas as a two-year-old at the Newmarket July Sales

collection of 79 stallions, mares, foals, yearlings and horses-in-training realized a total of 111,790 guineas. It included the three-year-old colt Harvester, bought by Sir John Willoughby for 8500 guineas, who proceeded to dead-heat with St Gatien in the Derby; and the three-year-old filly Busybody, bought by Mr George Baird for 8800 guineas, who won the 1000 Guineas and the Oaks.

The death of Baird seven years later led to another big dispersal sale, conducted by Tattersalls in two drafts with total receipts of 52,612 guineas. The star attraction was the unbeaten Meddler, whose three victories as a two-year-old in 1892 had included the Dewhurst plate, at the First July Sales the following year. Meddler was knocked down for 14,500 guineas, then a record for a thoroughbred at public auction, for export to the United States, where he became champion sire twice.

Towards the end of his career Edmund Tattersall began to take life more easily. By the autumn of 1896 his health was failing and he was persuaded to stay at home when the weather was inclement. However, despite the protests of his wife, he was determined to go to Newmarket for the Houghton Meeting, where he visited his great friend Mathew Dawson. Taken ill two days later, he returned to his south Kensington home, Coleherne Court, virtually an invalid. He never left the house again, but lived for another 18 months until his death on 5 March 1898.

Edmund Somerville Tattersall, 1863–1942

Edmund Somerville Tattersall was born on 12 August 1863 at the old house at Hyde Park Corner. He was the eldest son of Edmund Tattersall, a man of forty-eight at the time of his son's birth, and his wife Elizabeth. Shortly after Somerville was born his father had bought Coleherne Court, where the Tattersall children were brought up surrounded by the usual staff of cooks, nursery maids and servants associated with contemporary upper-middle-class families. As a result of a broad education Somerville blossomed into a young man of charm, taste and culture. Somewhat shy, and with a quiet

Somerville Tattersall (1863–1942) – the last of the dynasty

well-modulated voice, he developed a love of music and quickly proved that he had a wonderful ear. His mother, herself an accomplished pianist, encouraged his musical talents, and also approved of her son's love of mountaineering, but Edmund's father was adamant that Edmund was a Tattersall and should enter the family firm. Nevertheless Edmund was happy at Coleherne Court, with its pleasant garden, and its tennis parties, dinner parties and musical evenings. The house was invariably filled with flowers, and there was always music to enjoy. Edmund Somerville Tattersall initially came into the limelight at the 1885 July Sales at Newmarket. He was on the rostrum awaiting the arrival of his famous father, when the first lot was brought into the Ring. His father appeared, but soon afterwards it was evident that he was not well. 'Sommy' stood anxiously by his side. Suddenly, his father's voice deserted him altogether, as the first of the Blankney yearlings was led into the ring. Sommy took the hammer, spread his catalogue calmly on the shelf in front of him and proceeded to sell without turning a hair. He was perfectly self-possessed, persuasive of voice, patient and composed in the inevitable moments when bids hung fire. His sang-froid and, which was equally important, his familiarity with the pedigrees he read out, and his knack of never missing a bid, impressed his audience throughout the proceedings.

The Sales ring scene in the Park Paddocks in the 1890s

Moreover, he effected a good sale. The ten Hermits sold for 16,460 guineas, achieving an excellent average for the time. Sommy had made a good start and it was no surprise when he was made a partner before the end of the year. During the next 15 years he was to conduct many important sales, culminating in the dispersal sale of the late Duke of Westminster's horses at Kingsclere on 8 March 1900. Nineteen lots were sold for 70,440 guineas. The Triple Crown winner Flying Fox was bought by the French breeder Edmund Blanc for 37,500 guineas, which eclipsed Meddler's price and stood for 67 years as a record price for a horse in training. Four months later a number of the Duke of Westminster's broodmares and all his yearlings were sold at Newmarket, with Sommy becoming involved with Robert Standish Sievier. Soldier, actor, racehorse owner, professional backer, journalist and charlatan, Sievier had played a more than colourful part in English Turf affairs during the late 1890s. In the year in question, 1900, he had won about £30,000 over Diamond Jubilee's Derby; by the end of that eventful week he was about £53,000 to the good. On the evening preceding the Yearling Sales at Newmarket, Bob walked into the Rutland Arms Hotel and asked to see Mr Somerville Tattersall. 'I am going to buy the Persimmon filly out of Ornament,' he told him. 'As I have no account with you,' he continued, 'I thought you might like a deposit.'

'Not at all,' protested Sommy, smiling and holding out his hand. Into it, to his astonishment, was thrust £20,000 in Bank of England notes. 'It is far too much,' said Sommy, 'and I don't know what to do with so much money at this time of night.'

Anyway, there was the money, and it was getting late. Bob Sievier wished his host good evening, and Sommy went to his room.

The Rutland Arms, then as now, was a very respectable hotel, but Newmarket in race week sheltered many disreputable characters, and poor Sommy was not at all happy about the safe keeping of so large a sum of money. He peered around the room and finally hid the notes at the top of a wardrobe. He could hardly wait until Barclay's Bank opened the following morning, when he took the notes and handed them over to the manager with a sigh of relief. Shortly afterwards, the sale began.

It is Turf history that after a prolonged duel with the trainer

Sceptre, the winner of four Classic races. She was purchased by Mr Robert Sievier for the then fabulous price of 10,000 guineas as a yearling at the Newmarket July Sales

John Porter, acting for the new Duke of Westminster, Sievier acquired the Persimmon filly for 10,000 guineas, a price which exceeded the existing record for a yearling by 4000 guineas. Already named Sceptre, she became one of the greatest racemares of all time and won all the Classic races with the exception of the Derby.

In 1904 Sommy took a flat at 34 Rutland Gate, close to his business premises, and even nearer to his beloved Albert Hall. Despite his amazing industry and stamina, he could not manage on his own. When he was away from the office his younger brothers Harry George and Rupert administered the affairs of the partnership. However, in 1905 Sommy and Harry George quarrelled and Sommy accepted his brother's resignation. To assist the two remaining Tattersall brothers Gerald Deane was brought into the business, though not as a partner until after the First World War.

As early as the autumn of 1904 Deane took his share of work on the rostrum at Knightsbridge, and shortly afterwards

Polymelus, bought by Mr Solly Joel for 4200 guineas as a four-year-old at Newmarket in September 1906. He became leading sire of winners five times

graduated to more responsible duties at Newmarket and Doncaster. Not that Sommy allowed anyone but himself to deal with the most important lots. He was quite indefatigable and, on some occasions, stayed on the rostrum for the whole of a four-day sale – a feat of exceptional endurance, both mental and physical.

Another of the firm's auctioneers was J. R. Rawlence, the Secretary of the Masters of Foxhounds Association. He was at no time a partner in the firm, but sold frequently at Knightsbridge; his particular niche in the firm's activities was in conducting the annual hound sales at Rugby. Tattersall rented special premises for this sale, which, for a time, showed a good return; but it was abandoned shortly before the First World War.

When war broke out in August 1914, Sommy was obliged to carry on without an active partner. Gerald Deane had been recalled from the Reserve. He ended his service as a Major in command of the Remount Depot in Calais and did not return to the business until the war was over.

One of the greatest events in the history of Tattersalls in the period between the two World Wars was the dispersal of the bloodstock of the newspaper magnate Sir Edward Hulton at the Newmarket Second July Sales in 1925. Hulton had died in May, and it was an open secret that his mares, foals, yearlings and horses-in-training had been valued for probate at £150,000. This figure was considered far too high by some bloodstock experts, who thought £100,000 nearer the mark. In fact 77 lots were sold for £288,380 guineas, more than double the sum realized by the previous record dispersal, that of Lord Falmouth's bloodstock 61 years earlier. The mares included the Classic winners Fifinella and Straitlace in addition to Silver Tag, second in the One Thousand Guineas and third in the Oaks; Roselet, third in the Oaks: Shrove, third in the One Thousand Guineas and second in the Oaks; and Soubriquet, second in both the One Thousand Guineas and the Oaks. The top price was realized by the four-year-old Straitlace, winner of the Oaks, who was in foal to Lemberg and was bought for 17,000 guineas for export to France. The six-year-old Soubriquet, destined to be the great-granddam of the Derby winner Pinza, realized 12,500 guineas, and the wartime Derby and Oaks winner Fifinella realized 500 guineas less.

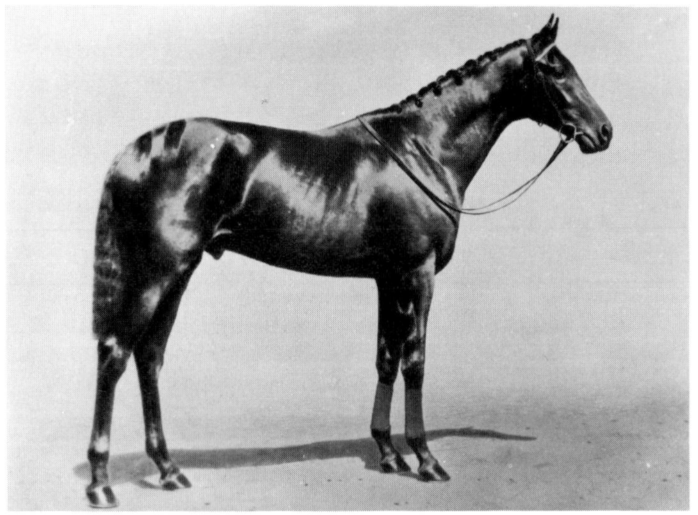

Solario, winner of the St Leger in 1925. He was bought for the record sum of 47,000 guineas by a syndicate of British breeders headed by Lords Glanely and Rosebery as a ten-year-old stallion at the Newmarket July Sales in 1932

There was another sensational sale seven years later when the ten-year-old stallion Solario was submitted at the Newmarket Second July Sales as part of the dispersal of the late Sir John Rutherford's bloodstock. Solario, who had won the St Leger, the Coronation Cup and the Ascot Gold Cup, had already proved himself as a stallion by siring the Classic colts Orpen and Dastur. Most of the experts valued him at no more than 40,000 guineas, but the bidding soared above that figure as a result of the competition between an American syndicate and a British syndicate headed by Lord Glanely and Lord Rosebery. In the end the British bidders prevailed at 47,000 guineas, a new record for a thoroughbred at public auction.

Solario had been bought by Sir John Rutherford for 3500 guineas at Tattersall's Doncaster September Sales as a yearling. He was only one of the many future Classic winners to be sold by Tattersalls in the period between the two World Wars. The others included the Derby winners Windsor Lad, who also won the St Leger, Papyrus, Manna, Blenheim and April the Fifth; the 2000 Guineas winners St Louis, Flamingo, Diolite and Colombo; the 1000 Guineas winners Four Course and Brown Betty; the Oaks winners Love in Idleness, Brownhylda, Straitlace, Rose of England and Lovely Rosa; and the St Leger winners Salmon Trout, Sandwich and Scottish Union.

Thus the quality of the horses sold by Tattersalls was extremely high. Nevertheless the racing and breeding scene was fraught with anxieties during the 1920s and 1930s, with consequent violent fluctuations in bloodstock prices. Yearling

Embossed hammer presented to Somerville Tattersall. It had been used by him for the record-breaking sale of Solario

prices soared to record levels in the boom immediately following the First World War, but fell back in the early 1920s. During this period the strongest force sustaining the market was the persistent buying of the Aga Khan, who was laying the foundations of a racing and breeding empire mainly by the purchase of choicely bred yearling fillies, though he also purchased a number of yearling colts like those destined to be the 2000 Guineas winner Diophon and the St Leger winner Salmon Trout. He entered the market in 1921, when his purchases at the Doncaster St Leger Sales amounted to eight yearlings for 24,520 guineas and an average of 3065 guineas, at a time when the average price of all yearlings at those sales was only 649 guineas. His purchases at the same sales the next year included the grey filly by The Tetrarch out of Lady Josephine for 9200 guineas, the highest price for a yearling filly since Sceptre had realized the record 10,000 guineas 22 years earlier. This filly by The Tetrarch, given the name of Mumtaz Mahal, possessed brilliant speed, her coruscating performances gaining her the soubriquet of 'The Flying Filly'. She also became the greatest of the Aga Khan's foundation mares, and her family has run like a continuous thread through the breeding operations of her purchaser and his son and grandson, who carried on his studs with striking success. Shergar, the magnificent but ill-fated Derby winner of 1981, was one of the legion of her distinguished descendants in the direct female line.

Yearling prices, generally speaking, recovered gradually; they reached a new peak in 1928, only to plunge in the aftermath of the financial crash the following year. As the slump continued and the threat of war grew in the 1930s, confidence remained at a low ebb, and prices never recovered the 1928 level before the outbreak of the Second World War. In 1933 business was so depressed that Tattersalls' staff salaries were cut by 15%, and Sommy was forced to sell his racehorses and forgo his entertainment allowance of £100 a month.

By 1939 Sommy was an old man, and much of the auctioneering and direction of the firm's affairs had passed to his partners Gerald Deane, Robert Needham and Terence Watt. The war brought severe restrictions on racing and the collapse of the bloodstock market. Moreover Sommy did not stand up well to the nervous and physical strain of the air raids on London, and his health deteriorated. He had a series of small strokes before his death on 26 October 1942.

Part Two

1

The Personalities in the First Half of the Twentieth Century

THE evolution of the House of Tattersall, its supremacy among the bloodstock auction houses of Britain and its eminence among the bloodstock auction houses of the world, have depended to an overwhelming degree upon the personalities of the men who have guided its fortunes during the two centuries of its existence. This may be a truism; but it cannot be too strongly emphasized that the success or failure of an auctioneering house springs from the contacts of the small number of men on the rostrum with their many clients, both sellers and buyers, and the ability of the auctioneers to inspire confidence in this three-cornered relationship. In the late twentieth century people in the world of racing and breeding tend to take Tattersalls for granted as the principal market for thoroughbreds. But it should not be forgotten that when the first Richard Tattersall founded his business of selling horses and hounds at Hyde Park Corner in 1766 he had plenty of competitors, some already well established, and there was nothing inevitable about the emergence of Tattersalls with a commanding lead in this specialized field. That it did so emerge, and afterwards maintained and increased that lead as the weight of the firm's business shifted gradually and at last exclusively to thoroughbreds, was due to the flair, industry, integrity and sheer professional competence of the founder and his successors – members of the Tattersall family until the end of the nineteenth century, Somerville Tattersall and his partners for most of the first half of the twentieth century and, in the second half of the twentieth century, men of new families who have been careful to preserve the best of the Tattersalls traditions while introducing the changes necessary to meet the formidable challenge of an unprecedented escalation of the value and the volume of the trade in thoroughbreds.

There is no doubt that the first Richard Tattersall exploited his charm and his command of the social graces, as well as his honesty and his acumen, in the interests of his business. He used lavish hospitality quite deliberately to cultivate the friendship of grandees like the Prince of Wales, the Duke of Kingston and Earl Grosvenor, who were potentially the biggest spenders among his customers. He was something of a social climber; there are less complimentary phrases in modern usage to describe that aspect of his activities. But any man is entitled to be judged by the standards and circumstances of his own time, not by the standards of a much later age. It is difficult now to visualize the deference and the privileges which were enjoyed by the nobility in the eighteenth century. Peers were above the laws that applied to commoners. They could run up huge debts without fear of arrest; they could commit criminal offences, and no ordinary court had jurisdiction over them. To ignore such men was folly: not to take positive steps to attract them commercial suicide. The patronage of the nobility was crucial to the success of an enterprise like Richard Tattersall's, and the hospitality that he extended to them, in addition to the provision of the Subscription Room and its amenities, played the same part in the early development of Tattersalls as advertisement and public relations play in the promotion of any successful business in the late twentieth century.

The dominance of the nobility in the world of the horse, and especially of the thoroughbred, two centuries ago is indicated clearly by the list of subscribers to the annual *Racing Calendar* of 1780. They included one royal Duke (Eclipse's breeder the Duke of Cumberland), thirteen other Dukes, two Marquises, twenty-two Earls, two Viscounts and twenty-four other lords. Even as late as 1893 the list of members of Tattersall's Subscription Room at Albert Gate included one Russian Prince, three Dukes, three Marquises, seven Earls and six other lords – and they, it may be surmised, were only those members of the nobility who had an active and regular interest in betting on racehorses. However, by the end of the nineteenth century the democratization of British society was well advanced, and the House of Tattersall had undisputed pre-eminence in its own field of business and no call to curry favour with anybody.

This pre-eminence had been demonstrated by the case of the Cobham Stud Company 14 years earlier. The ailing company decided to dispense with the services of Tattersalls at the annual sale of yearlings held at the stud, and employed in their place an auctioneer named Rymill, who was unknown to the racing community. William Allison, a racing journalist and director of the company, described the outcome in his memoirs, *My Kingdom for a Horse*:

> Buyers fought shy, and the total realised for 56 yearlings was only 10,700 guineas, not half the 22,070 guineas which had been totalled at the sale of the year before. Such a drop as this coming on top of an already dubious financial situation was fatal, and whenever I hear people complaining of Messrs. Tattersall's monopoly as auctioneers of bloodstock I always call to mind that one object-lesson.

The outcome of this rash and ill-judged decision was that the company was forced into liquidation. And if the Cobham Stud sale demonstrated that the services of Tattersalls were indispensable in the quality thoroughbred market, the returns of bloodstock sales, which were published in the annual issues of the *Racing Calendar* from 1894, provided equally conclusive evidence of the grip of Tattersalls on the quantity market. For example, in 1898, the year of Somerville Tattersall's accession to the senior partnership, Tattersalls sold 1582, or 72% of the total of 2209 head of bloodstock sold at auction in England, and had an unchallengeable lead over other reputable firms like Fords, Stevens and Sheldons. In respect of yearlings, the most essential commodity in commercial thoroughbred breeding, Tattersalls had a virtual monopoly.

Somerville Tattersall, the last Tattersall to be head of the firm, had all the charm of his predecessors allied to an independence of spirit appropriate to the firm's assured position in the bloodstock world. He was a man of first-class intellect. He was the top classical scholar at Eton, and on leaving school went to an academy at Vevey, on the Lake of

Geneva, and afterwards spent a year in Dresden, becoming fluent in both French and German. In Switzerland, too, he learned to love mountains, skiing and mountaineering. In later years he had many holidays in Switzerland, and climbed the Matterhorn twice and the Jungfrau once. His mountaineering dress was eccentric if utilitarian, consisting of a belted jacket of thick tweed with buttoned pockets, baggy knickerbocker trousers of the same material, brown woollen ribbed stockings, hobnailed boots and a peaked cap with ear-flaps. He wore the same outfit for early morning visits to the gallops when Tattersalls owned the Manton training establishment in the 1920s and 1930s. So attired, he must have been a quaint sight in Knightsbridge when he stepped into his chauffeur-driven Chrysler at 5.00 a.m. for his expeditions to Wiltshire.

His sporting activities were matched by his artistic tastes. He loved painting, and was an ardent follower of the theatre and a member of the Garrick Club. However, his passion was music. Although he did not play an instrument, he had a wonderful ear and was a Vice-President of the Royal Academy of Music for many years. Sir Edward Elgar, Sir Henry Wood and Sir Yehudi Menuhin were among his close friends. He attended the great violin virtuoso's first London appearance with the San Francisco orchestra in 1929, and missed none of his concerts in London before the Second World War.

Somerville Tattersall with Yehudi Menuhin and his two sisters in the garden of the Menuhin family's house near Paris

He stayed with the Menuhin family at their home at Aille d'Avray near Paris and became very fond of Yehudi and his sisters Hepzibah and Yalta. More than forty years after Sommy's death Sir Yehudi wrote of him:

> He [Sommy] was one of our dearest friends and that included the whole family – my mother, father and sisters. I cannot remember on what occasion we made his acquaintance but he was, for us, the epitome of the British gentleman.
>
> As you can imagine, it was a great novelty for us to learn about the tradition that Tattersalls represents. We knew little about horses and loved not only the novelty but the warmth and friendship. I remember lunching with him, with the whole family, and that was the first time I saw grape scissors and was amazed, coming from California, to observe how precious these wonderful hot-house bunches were. We loved him dearly and we seemed to fill some niche in his heart for he never failed to see us or invite us when we came to London.

Somerville was a man of deep religious faith and a church-warden at Holy Trinity Church, Brompton, for many years. He was also a true Christian in his daily life and personal relationships, for he was extremely kind and generous, especially to the children of his friends and relatives, plying them with chocolates from Fortnum and Mason, loading them with presents at birthdays and Christmas-time and reciting humorous verses to them with irresistible comic gusto. One of his favourites ran:

Johnny Morgan's
Nasal organ
Turned a purple blue.
He to hide it
Went and dyed it
To its natural hue.
In the night
It was quite all right
But in the day . . . . Oh My!
A horrid blotch
Of special Scotch
Kept peeping through the dye.

The cynical may object, not without some justice, that attitudes of constant benevolence towards children come more easily to godparents and honorary uncles, who see them only occasionally and on their best behaviour, than to the actual parents who, besides enjoying their sunny moods, have also to endure their inevitable tears, tantrums and irrationality. Nevertheless it would be both churlish and untruthful to deny to Sommy the credit for a constant and genuine fondness for children. Angela Thorne, one of the two daughters of his partner Gerald Deane – her elder sister Iris was actually his god-daughter, but he was equally fond of the spirited Angela – remembered all her life how, when she was a small girl, Sommy used to pick her up, put her on his shoulders with one leg dangling on each side of his neck, and take her for walks. One of her abiding memories was of a Sunday morning after church when they were in Hyde Park opposite the Dorchester Hotel. An open landau drawn by two bays was approaching, with two ladies in close-fitting black toque hats sitting in the back. With Angela still perched on his shoulders, Sommy swept off his black topper as they passed, and the two ladies turned towards him and bowed. 'That was Queen Alexandra and her sister,' he told her. He was devoted to the Queen, and kept a silver-framed photograph of her on his writing-table.

Sommy's outfit of topper and frock coat for a Sunday morning stroll in Hyde Park exemplified his strict sense of decorum. Despite his tapering shoulders, which must have posed problems for his tailors, and his walrus moustache, he exuded an air of old-world elegance that was most evident on great racing occasions like Derby Day and Royal Ascot, when he was immaculate in shining black top hat, black morning coat, pin-striped trousers and Old Etonian tie asserted by a pearl tie-pin. He always gave a party for the Derby, at which the ladies were presented with bunches of pink carnations and the gentlemen with one carnation each for their buttonholes.

Although he never married, he was always an admirer of beautiful women and is known to have made at least one proposal of marriage. He remarked sadly in later life: 'Alice was very beautiful, but she chose to marry Charles Cotesworth.' She was tall, slim and very fair with blue eyes, and her beauty seemed as exquisite but as devoid of vitality as Dresden china – the kind to excite admiration but not passion. Sommy probably admired her in the same way as he admired all beauty whether in art or nature. On the other hand, he enjoyed intensely the company of attractive and lively young women, and showered them with presents of fur coats, jewellery and other expensive adornments.

He also enjoyed the company of personable young men. For a number of years he used to stay with the Provost of Eton for the Royal Ascot meetings, and on one of those visits he made the acquaintance of an exceptionally good-looking boy in 'Toddy' Vaughan's house. The boy, Gerald Deane, was already fascinated by horses and racing, and was in recurrent trouble on account of his addiction to reading the scurrilous racing novels of Nat Gould both in and out of school. Their shared interest in racing drew Sommy and Gerald together, and they quickly formed a close friendship which lasted until Sommy's death more than 40 years later.

After leaving Eton Gerald Deane was gazetted to the 11th Hussars, and at the age of nineteen was posted to Egypt as ADC to General 'Bully' Oliphant. It must have seemed an ideal first posting for a subaltern of sporting tastes, but it was cut short when he was admitted to the Citadel Hospital in Cairo with rheumatic fever and pernicious anaemia. He became so seriously ill that his mother travelled out by sea to be with him. She was accompanied by the faithful Sommy Tattersall.

When Gerald had turned the corner and was on the road to recovery his future became the subject of debate. Sommy urged him to abandon a military career which had started so inauspiciously, and to join him in the firm. This was not an idea which his family could readily accept. Gerald's father Arthur Deane came from an old Hampshire family and was a director of the family's private bank Deane and Littlehales; he was Master of the Hursley Hounds and farmed 600 acres at Littleton, 2 miles north-west of Winchester. To his mind, leaving a famous cavalry regiment to become an auctioneer involved a definite loss of caste. A tug-of-war developed. But Sommy, for all his quiet voice and gentle manner, could be extremely persuasive. Moreover Gerald Deane was a strong-willed young man perfectly capable of making his own decisions. When the options were soldiering and a job which would bring him into constant touch with the world of racing, where his heart really lay, there was no doubt on which side the scales would fall. Parental prejudice was swept aside and he decided to leave the army and accept Sommy's invitation. He joined the firm as an assistant on 1 May 1904 at a salary of £500 per year, which was increased to £1200 three years later. £200 of this salary was paid by Sommy out of his own pocket.

Sommy's motives for recruiting Gerald may have been ambivalent at the outset, but his instinct for choosing the right man to further the interests of Tattersalls certainly did not betray him. If the first requirement in an auctioneer is the ability to attract and hold the attention of his audience, then Gerald Deane fulfilled it to a marked degree. On the rostrum his looks, his firm but delicately chiselled profile, his strong jaw, wavy brown hair and reddish moustache of military style, made him the cynosure of all eyes. His dynamic personality could be spell-binding. His voice was vibrant, his tone often impatient, his manner sometimes aggressive. 'I can't dwell: quick, or you lose him', he would rap out to a hesitant underbidder. He was the perfect counterbalance to the rostrum persona of Sommy Tattersall. Where Sommy coaxed, Gerald shocked the bidder into action. In addition, Gerald was a first-class judge of a horse, and a fine horseman and rider to hounds, spending the rest of the winter hunting with the Pytchley and the Warwickshire when the December Sales were over.

It was not until February 1922, more than three years after his return as a Major from First World War service with the Remounts, that Gerald was taken into partnership by Sommy, but from that moment the base of their joint operations rapidly broadened. A month later Lord Manton died of a heart attack while out hunting with the Warwickshire Hounds. He was the owner of the training establishment from which he had taken his title, and had built up a powerful stud and racing string. His executors decided to dispose of the bloodstock forthwith, but Sommy intervened to lease five of the fillies-in-training. The intervention had a happy outcome for both parties, because the fillies earned more than £22,000 in prize money, of which Sommy received half, and appreciated considerably in value so that they realized the aggregate sum of 41,700 guineas when they were submitted at the December Sales the following year. They included Tetrabbazia, who was destined to be the dam of the St Leger winner Singapore, and Lady Juror, who had proved herself one of the best-staying fillies-in-training by carrying Sommy's colours to victory in the Jockey Club Stakes over 1¾ miles. Later she gained undying fame as the dam of the brilliant racehorse and champion sire Fair Trial.

From left to right: Somerville Tattersall, Alec Taylor, Lord Astor and Gerald Deane. Taylor trained for all the other three men at Manton

The lease of these fillies strengthened a connection with their training stable Manton which had been initiated by the post-war appointment of Gerald Deane as racing manager to Lord Astor. Waldorf Astor and Gerald had known each other at Eton, brought together by their shared interest in racing in spite of the gap of 3 years in their ages. Astor had had horses in training at Manton since 1911, and his Cliveden Stud had developed into one of the most select thoroughbred nurseries in England. A gentle and intensely loyal man, he turned naturally to an old friend for professional assistance in the task of managing a large number of horses in training.

Whether Gerald's advice was sought on the finer points of stable policy is questionable. In the first place, he was mistrusted as too volatile and too much of a gambler by Astor's wife, the formidable Nancy, although Gerald and his first wife Kay were sometimes included in the Cliveden house parties in the 1920s. In the second place, Waldorf Astor himself had a consuming and exclusive interest in those of his horses that showed a touch of class, and was more inclined to listen to Alec Taylor and Joe Lawson, the successive trainers at Manton, and to his jockey Bobby Dick, who wrote him long and frequent letters concerning the progress of the horses, than to someone less closely involved with them. Between 1917 and 1945 he won a total of eleven Classic races; five of those victories were in the Oaks, a record which was partial compensation for his bad luck in the Derby, in which he had five seconds and not a single winner. He had no time at all for, and often gave away, any horse that fell below the high standard he demanded, and it seems that Gerald's duties were more concerned with the management and disposal of the inferior products of Cliveden, and the duller aspects of routine, rather than the strategy for the Classic and semi-Classic horses.

Nevertheless, the amount of work was considerable, and the association lasted until 1937. The reason then given for Gerald's retirement was ill health, and it was true that by then his symptoms of mental disturbance were increasingly evident. However, the ostensible was not the only reason, and the antipathy of Nancy Astor almost certainly contributed to the breach.

When Waldorf Astor sent his horses to Manton the trainer was Alec Taylor, the so-called 'Wizard of Manton' who was champion trainer twelve times and won no fewer than twenty-one Classic races. A partial recluse who seldom left the place except to go to the races or the sales, and never to take a holiday, Taylor originally owned Manton and 5000 acres of surrounding downland; he sold the property after the First World War, on condition that he should continue to train there until he decided to retire. He was the tenant of Lord Manton's executors for five years after the latter's death, but as Taylor's retirement at the end of the 1927 flat season approached it became known that the executors were anxious to sell the property. As there were no other buyers in sight, Sommy Tattersall and Gerald Deane stepped in and bought it for Tattersalls, thus forging the closest possible link between the principal bloodstock auctioneering house and one of the foremost training stables in Britain. The training was taken over by Joe Lawson, who had been head lad to Alec Taylor and proved just as successful as his old master. Like Taylor and Sommy Tattersall, Joe Lawson was a lifelong bachelor and a thorough professional.

In this way the Tattersalls connection with Manton had acquired several different strands. There was the outright ownership of the stables, gallops and downs; there was Gerald's management of the horses bred and owned by the stable's most illustrious patron, Lord Astor; and there was the ownership by Sommy and Gerald, sometimes as partners, of numerous horses trained in the stable. Sommy had owned a few horses, with limited success, as a young man under the name of 'Mr Preston', when owners were permitted to use pseudonyms without infringing the Rules of Racing. However, his colours (pink, brown sleeves, black cap) were in moth-balls for many years after he became head of the firm. His successful venture in leasing fillies from Lord Manton's executors encouraged him to take a more active part in racehorse ownership, and from the mid-1920s to the Second World War he won nearly a hundred races. He never won a Classic race, but had a number of near misses. He had three placed horses in the Derby: Hurstwood finished third in 1924, Brienz third in 1929 and Iliad, beaten by no more than a length by Blenheim, came second the following year. His other horses placed in Classic races were Foliation, third in the St Leger in 1926; Flegere, third in the Oaks two years later; and Thorndean, second in the 1000 Guineas in 1932. Foliation was probably the best of all his horses. That top-class filly won eight races, including three afterwards classified as Group 2 Pattern races – the Nassau Stakes, the Ribblesdale Stakes and the Hardwicke Stakes.

Sommy was less prominent as a breeder, though he owned Sceptre, that mare of immortal reputation, for a time. He bought her as a twelve-year-old at the December Sales in 1911 to prevent her being exported, but sold her to the Melton Stud 3 years later. She bred him one winner, Grosvenor, whose solitary success was gained in the Great Foal Stakes at Newmarket as a three-year-old.

Gerald's racehorses were less numerous and generally of lower class than those of Sommy. The best of them was Braishfield, whom he bought and renamed after he had run for Lady James Douglas as 8th Division as a two-year-old. Braishfield was a colt of class and versatility, winning the Sussex Stakes over a mile at Goodwood and the Great Yorkshire Stakes over 1½ miles at York within the space of a month as a three-year-old. At Goodwood he beat Sarchedon, who had been fourth in the Derby, and Caligula, who went on to win the St Leger. The next year he won the Churchill Stakes over 2 miles at Royal Ascot, and a month later finished second to Lord Astor's Craig An Eran in the Eclipse Stakes over 1¼ miles at Sandown. It must be admitted that the Eclipse Stakes was a one-sided contest as Craig An Eran, who started at 7–2 on, beat Braishfield by 5 lengths without ever coming off the bridle.

Another notable horse to carry Gerald's colours (light blue with pink hooped sleeves and very similar to Waldorf Astor's light blue with pink sash and cap) was the game little mare Blackness, whom he bought for £500 and a load of hay. The finest achievement of Blackness was to land a gamble in the Derby Cup, then one of the principal autumn handicaps, in November 1927. Gerald used the proceeds of the gamble to build a range of boxes, which were known as 'the Blackness boxes', at the Littleton Stud, which he had inherited from his father. The material value of his association with Astor was demonstrated by the fact that Astor sent Craig An Eran, who won the 2000 Guineas as well as the Eclipse Stakes, and another of his good horses Buchan, who won the Eclipse Stakes twice, to stand as stallions at Littleton. In 1925 Buchan and Craig An Eran stood at fees of 400 guineas and 250 guineas respectively, and were among the highest-priced stallions in the country. Each left a considerable mark on the Stud Book.

The Tattersalls team of auctioneers had been increased by the recruitment of Robert Needham in August 1920 at a salary of £700 a year. Needham had served in the R H A during the war, but was an Australian by birth. Born in 1891, he had worked as a jackaroo in Queensland as a young man, and was very proud of his skill at cracking a very long stock-whip. He was equally proud of his father, who had sailed round the world before the mast in windjammers. He had great respect for physical prowess. His bullet-shaped head, strong chin and long straight nose were the physical counterparts of his mental toughness and uncompromising demeanour. He was not highly educated, lacked a finely developed sense of humour and was weak in aesthetic appreciation.

These traits suggested that Bob Needham was poles apart from the cultured Sommy Tattersall in character. Nevertheless his recruitment proved a wise choice, for he possessed many sterling qualities to compensate for his limitations. Most importantly, he was an excellent auctioneer, firm, patient and persuasive. He was scrupulously honest, and inspired absolute confidence in everyone with whom he had dealings. He was exceptionally hard-working and an indefatigable compiler of statistics relating to the sales and the bloodstock industry. He was always willing to give advice and to share his knowledge with anyone who sought his help. To sum up, he had a strong and resourceful personality which was the rock on which the fortunes of the firm rested during the difficult days of the Second World War.

Bob Needham entered the firm as a salaried member of the staff, and it was not until March 1936 that he was taken into partnership. The partnership agreement specified that he was to receive a salary of £1500 a year, while the profits were to be distributed as to 68/100ths to Sommy Tattersall, 27/100ths to Gerald Deane and 5/100ths to himself. The agreement made it clear that although the firm was formally a partnership, the real power remained in the hands of Sommy. The relevant clause stated that Sommy was to have 'sole direction of the said business and all matters connected therewith including engagement and dismissal of all clerks and others employed, ... If any difference of question touching the conduct of the business shall arise between the partners the views of Edmund Somerville Tattersall shall prevail and his decision shall be binding on the other partners.'

The agreement also laid down that 'each of the partners shall at all times faithfully and diligently employ himself on partnership affairs'. However, large concessions were made to the many outside interests of Gerald Deane, for the agreement stated that he was 'at liberty to carry on for his own profit and advantage' the following activities:

1. His stud and agricultural farms at Littleton.
2. The management of Lord Astor's horses-in-training.
3. His interest in the Priory Stud syndicate.
4. His directorship and management of Apelle Ltd.

Some of these interests may have made only small demands on his time. For example the Italian-bred Apelle, who had won the Coronation Cup as a five-year-old in 1928, stood at Littleton together with Buchan and Hurstwood. But they amounted to a heavy, and probably an excessive, work-load, which must surely have hastened the deterioration of his mental health.

Gerald Deane was at all times exceptionally mercurial, and his temper had a very low boiling-point. His condition was probably a legacy of the rheumatic fever of which he had so nearly died in Cairo as a very young man. The symptoms of manic depression began to manifest themselves within a few years of his return home, and his daughter Angela became aware of his abnormality soon after the First World War, when she was only eight. He had spells in which he became progressively more excitable, over-confident and overbearing, until he suddenly cracked without warning and plunged into depths of hopelessness in which he was unable to cope with the simplest matters of business or everyday life. In the depressive phases he showed strong suicidal tendencies, and at the age of fourteen Angela was sent with him to a hotel in Weymouth where he was to recuperate from one of his nervous breakdowns, with strict instructions not to let him shave or bathe in the sea alone, a terrible responsibility for so young a girl.

The illness settled into a cycle of about 2 years. In the manic phases he was prone to uncontrollable outbursts of temper and impulsive, eccentric and irrational behaviour. On one occasion during the Second World War he hired a car, drove it into the middle of a field near Littleton at four in the morning and sat in the back, with a loaded gun across his knees, saying that he was there to shoot a fox. He could be dangerous if thwarted. He regarded a particular corner seat on the morning train from Winchester to London's Waterloo Station, the route for his daily journeys from home to the office, as his by prescriptive right. One day he was exasperated to find on boarding the train that the seat was already occupied by a man who proceeded to aggravate his offence by filling the compartment with clouds of smoke from an evil-smelling pipe. Furious, Gerald opened the window and took the seat opposite. The offender rose and shut the window, and Gerald promptly opened it again. The battle of wills continued inconclusively until the offender went down the corridor to the lavatory, when Gerald, having noticed a loose nail lying fortuitously on the floor of the carriage, followed him and hammered the nail with his shoe through the wooden lavatory door and into the door-jamb, holding the door fast. Gerald returned to the compartment and occupied his usual seat, contentedly ignoring the pounding of fists and the angry shouts from the lavatory. In accordance with his habit of pursuing physical fitness, Gerald left the train at Clapham Junction to run or walk the three miles to Knightsbridge Green. On alighting he requested a porter to telephone ahead to Waterloo to warn the railway police that there was a madman on the train whom he had succeeded in imprisoning in the lavatory. As the train drew into Waterloo minutes later, two policemen boarded it, burst into the lavatory and marched Gerald's adversary away down the platform, deaf to his pleas that he was as sane as they were and the victim of a malicious practical joke.

Prominent members of the racing fraternity and clients of Tattersalls did not necessarily enjoy immunity from Gerald's outbreaks of temper, as an incident involving Martin Benson plainly testified. Benson was the founder of the bookmaking firm Douglas Stuart which advertised extensively in the 1930s under the slogan 'Duggie Never Owes'. He was also a racehorse owner and breeder on a substantial scale. He bought the Derby winner Windsor Lad during the summer of 1934 and won the St Leger with him, but his greatest claim to fame was his purchase of the Italian champion Nearco for £60,000 after he had won the Grand Prix de Paris in 1938. He installed the horse at his Beech House Stud at Newmarket, and Nearco became one of the most influential stallions in the history of the thoroughbred. Inevitably Benson's bloodstock operations involved him frequently in Tattersalls sales as buyer or vendor, and as a regular client of the firm for many years he was entitled to be treated with consideration. He was a dapper little man, sallow in complexion, with a neatly curled grey moustache, and much given to wearing cloth-topped boots or spats and a spotless grey Homburg. One day he called to see Gerald in his office at the top of the stairs at Knightsbridge Green. Presently the sounds of an altercation, with Gerald's voice ominously raised, began to come from the office. The noise reached a crescendo, and then the door was flung open and Benson came tumbling head over heels down the stairs. He picked himself up, apparently unhurt, and began to dust himself down. Within seconds there was the sound of a sash being violently raised upstairs and a grey Homburg was seen sailing into the yard, accompanied by Gerald's furious shout: 'And you can take your bloody hat with you, too!'

Partnership does not ensure harmony, and in the late 1930s

it was apparent that Gerald Deane and Bob Needham did not always see eye to eye. Nor did their wives, often a decisive factor in this kind of equation, get on well together. Gerald was married twice. His first wife, whom he married in 1907, was Kathleen (Kay) Rose, the lovely younger sister of Evelyn Fleming, whose sons Peter and Ian both became household names. By her he had two daughters: Iris, who married Brigadier Dominick Browne, and Angela, who married Major Brassey Thorne and became a distinguished artist, painting portraits of the Queen and the Duke of Edinburgh and of Queen Elizabeth the Queen Mother. Gerald's first marriage ended in divorce, and in 1930 he married Betty McKinnon, by whom he had a son Bruce, who followed him into the firm. It was his second wife Betty who clashed with Bob's wife Mona, the daughter of a British Admiral. Mona was a strong-willed woman whose influence had been effective in planing down the rough edges of her husband's personality, formed in the Australian outback.

In seeking fresh blood to bring into the firm Sommy was motivated partly by the need for a salve for this hostility between the Deanes and the Needhams. But this was not the only motive. Sommy was acutely conscious that he was growing old and that he was the last of the Tattersall dynasty, for he was adamant in his refusal to take his nephew Edmund, the son of his former partner Harry George and the only member of the family available, into the firm. He was convinced that it was essential to broaden the base of the partnership in order to secure its future, and it was with this idea that he approached his solicitors, Baileys Shaw and Gillett of Berners Street, to ask whether they could suggest somebody suitable. Baileys were also solicitors for the Bentinck family and, after consulting the head of the family the Duke of Portland, they put forward the name of Captain Terence Watt. As Sommy was an old friend of Captain Watt's father Sam Watt, a great horseman, the suggestion appealed to him strongly.

Terry Watt was related to the Bentincks, as his wife Alice was the second daughter of Lord Charles Cavendish Bentinck, a younger brother of the sixth Duke of Portland, who has a secure place in the annals of the Turf as the owner of the brilliant racehorse and stallion St Simon. Lord Charles did not aspire to the same prominence in racing, but had an honour-

Three stalwarts of Tattersalls in the middle of the twentieth century. From left to right: Terence Watt, Robert Needham and John Cherry

able career as soldier and sportsman. He served in the second Boer War, in which he was with the force besieged in Mafeking, and the First World War, in which he was a staff officer at Gallipoli. He was wounded in both wars and awarded the DSO in 1916. He played polo for the 9th Lancers, and at various times was Master of the Croome, the Blankney, the Burton and the Southwold Hounds. The Watt family, on the other hand, had been settled in Ireland since James I's plantation, and had acquired considerable properties in Londonderry and Donegal. Charles Bentinck was not an easy man to get to know, but he had no hesitation in recommending Terry as someone whose background and personality made him ideal for Tattersalls.

Terry Watt, who was born in 1906, was educated at Harrow and passed through Sandhurst before being commissioned in the 17th Lancers. However, he transferred subsequently to the Life Guards, because he wanted to marry and the 17th did not allow married subalterns. He was a keen shot, an excellent and versatile horseman, and a lover of all kinds of country pursuits. He played polo for both his regiments, was a brilliant man to hounds and a more than competent race rider in point-to-points and under National Hunt Rules. In the winter he hunted with the Cottesmore, the Fernie and the Belvoir and, as his sister Cecil McCullough recalled many years later: 'He was a pleasure to watch in the hunting field. He rode quietly and purposefully, and at the same time was gracious and understanding to all other followers of the hunt. Not that he always rode well-made horses, either. He rode lots of problem horses, but you would never know the difference.'

That same graciousness characterized all his personal relationships and was the key to his faculty for making and keeping friends in all walks of life, from grooms and ghillies to the grandees of the racing world. One of his closest friends was Anthony (afterwards Lord) Mildmay, the amateur rider famous for his association with horses like Cromwell and Davy Jones, with whom observers noted that he seemed to be on 'a special wavelength'.

While he was in the army Terry Watt enjoyed annual shooting and fishing holidays in Scotland during August and September. The holidays usually began with a visit to John Morrison (later Lord Margadale) on Islay, whence he would work his way across country to end up staying with the Portlands at Langwell on the east coast of Caithness. Nevertheless he became increasingly preoccupied with racing and race-riding. He owned a mare called Scissors, on whom he won fourteen races, mostly point-to-points but including the Household Brigade Hunters Challenge Cup, a 3½-mile steeplechase run at Hawthorn Hill. He also rode frequently for Colonel Gerald Foljambe, who trained jumpers at Buckminster in Leicestershire. The best horse in the stable was Donzelon, who alternated between hunter and regular chases with splendid impartiality. Terry Watt was not associated with Donzelon's biggest wins in the National Hunt Handicap Chase and the Scottish Grand National in 1929, but he did ride him to victory in hunter chases at Woore and Colwall Park two years later.

Drama is never far away where racing over fences is concerned, and Terry had more than his fair share of it when riding a horse called Ballybeg at the Fernie point-to-point. Terry's father was convinced that the horse would win and placed a big bet with one of the local bookies. Ballybeg was going well until he gave Terry a heavy fall at a fence out in the country. Terry lost his glasses and, after much groping around on the landing side of the fence, retrieved them intact but covered in mud. Nothing daunted, he remounted and, casualties having been wholesale among the other runners, went on to win the race. It seemed a happy outcome until Terry's father went to collect his winnings and found that the bookie had welshed.

Four years after his wins on Donzelon Terry resigned his

commission and took out a licence to train, first at Birkholme in Lincolnshire only 5 miles from Gerald Foljambe's stables, and later at West Ilsley on the Berkshire Downs near Newbury. He began with jumpers of modest ability, but his thoroughness and his way with horses and people were leading to gradual improvement of the stable's fortunes before the possibility of joining Tattersalls provided the prospect of branching out in a new and promising direction. Sam Watt, Terry and Cecil were invited down to Newmarket to have lunch with the Tattersalls partners in their private room. Sommy struck Cecil as charming and delightful, the epitome of an Edwardian gentleman. Sam and Sommy indulged in fluent reminiscences of men and horses, and the luncheon party passed off so agreeably that Cecil had to remind herself sharply that 'we were being looked over'. Evidently Sommy liked what he saw and heard of Terry, whose knowledge of horses and all the people in the horse world who came to buy and sell at Tattersalls fitted him perfectly for a job in the firm. Terry accepted an invitation to join Tattersalls as an assistant in October 1937.

More formal arrangements followed. A contract drawn up in February of the following year gave him an annual salary of £750, and his duties were defined as 'to conduct sales and any other work in the business as directed, with four weeks holiday'. However, that initial contract was superseded by a partnership agreement on 20 January 1939. Terry had to put £9000 in cash into the business, to form part of the £100,000 capital of Tattersalls, with Sommy contributing £45,000, Gerald £32,000 and Bob Needham £14,000. The profits were to be divided in the same proportions, but Bob was to continue to receive £1500 salary. Sommy retained the overriding control which had been spelt out in the 1936 partnership agreement.

Terry quickly established a reputation as an efficient auctioneer and an asset to the firm. His sense of humour was lively and dry, sometimes sardonic, but seldom expressed in ways that gave offence. On the contrary, his enviable talent for making friends and the respect in which he was held in the horse world made him readily acceptable to Tattersalls' clientele in his new role. The bloodstock market had remained flat throughout the 1930s, for any hopes of recovery from the financial crash of 1929 were thwarted by the growing threat of another world war. In 1938 prices at the premier yearling sales, the Doncaster St Leger Sales, did not even reach the level of 1920, let along the record level of 1928. However, Tattersalls had developed a strong and broadly based team, and were well placed to profit if the world political situation were to take a more favourable turn. Unhappily, more optimistic forecasts were dashed by the outbreak of war in September 1939 and the consequent collapse of the bloodstock market. In the next few years the fortunes of Tattersalls were to sink to a low ebb, not only through the inevitable severe curtailment of wartime racing and breeding, but also through the incidence of death and illness that devastated the partnership.

2
Kenneth Rupert Watt

TERRY Watt rejoined the army on the outbreak of war. In 1940 he was given command of a squadron of the Phantom GHQ liaison regiment stationed in Northern Ireland, but on 17 July 1942 he died of shock and severe multiple injuries when the light aeroplane in which he was flying on active service crashed in a field near Ruthin in the mountains of North Wales. Sommy Tattersall himself died 3 months later.

A somewhat bland and banal obituary notice was printed in the correspondence columns of *The Times* shortly after Terry's death, stating: 'He was a most efficient officer; his loss is a severe one for his regiment and also for his firm.'

Phantom would have had a crucial role in the event of a German attempt to occupy the Irish Republic, and many years later Derek Hignett, the regimental commander at the time, made a much more reflective and penetrating observation when he remarked during a conversation with Cecil McCullough: 'You know, when I commanded Phantom I could pick exactly whom I wanted as officers. They had to be people who were used to riding their own line, as it were.'

And, in reporting the conversation, Mrs McCullough added: 'And that is exactly what described Terry. In his own quiet way, whether it was in the hunting field or in a race or through life, I think he rode his own line with a smile.'

The esteem in which Terry was held by all ranks is demonstrated by the fact that when his body was taken home by ambulance it was accompanied by an escort of troopers of his regiment at their own urgent request. He was buried at Exton, three miles from Oakham, whose tiny church he had attended since boyhood and for which he had a special affection.

The almost simultaneous deaths of Sommy and Terry left a huge gap in the partnership of Tattersalls, and the remaining partners began to look round for a replacement with something like desperation. In the long term an obvious candidate might be Terry's only son Michael, but he was a small boy of only nine. A close relation of Terry, his first cousin Captain Kenneth Watt, was the right age and in the right place, because he was commanding the cavalry squadron of Cambridge University Officer Training Corps and was living in Cambridge, only 12 miles from Newmarket. In the autumn of 1942 the partners extended an invitation to him to join them on trial and, after some hesitation, he agreed. Ken Watt did his first stint of auctioneering at the December Sales the same year.

The advent of Ken Watt was one of the most momentous happenings in the history of Tattersalls, for he was to be the true architect of the firm's fortunes in the period of astonishingly rapid evolution of the bloodstock industry in the second half of the twentieth century. He brought a marvellous array of qualities to the service of the firm, enabling it to survive an early series of management crises and then inspiring changes and adaptations during his thirty years as senior partner and chairman which transformed the previous somewhat fusty image of Tattersalls and rendered it equal to all the challenges of the modern world in which the thoroughbred became a prime international commodity.

He possessed some outstanding natural advantages. He had shining and seemingly ageless good looks, added to a native charm and an unforced courtesy of manner which his distinguished predecessor Sommy Tattersall surely would have approved, though his tone of voice was more incisive than Sommy's. He had immense determination and moral courage, a transparent integrity which won him universal trust, a respect for tradition combined with an imaginative insight into the needs of the future, a well-developed aesthetic sense, great loyalty to friends and colleagues, and a driving ambition to expand the business of Tattersalls and maintain its leadership among European bloodstock auctioneering houses. All these attributes were united with the skill of a first-class auctioneer. Tony Morris, the leading thoroughbred breeding journalist for more than half Ken's chairmanship, shrewdly observed in an article published in the *Sporting Life* on 7 December 1982:

I can state sincerely that it was always a privilege to watch him at work – an accomplished practitioner of the traditional style with a thorough knowledge of horses and the market.

He was never the flamboyant exhibitionist, unlike some who seem to be angling for an engagement at the London Palladium, but his mastery of the art was complete and his technique flawless – aside from those occasions when he failed to disguise his irritation over a reserve pitched absurdly high.

Morris's tribute was true and generous, and he might have added that Ken's irritation over reserves pitched absurdly high was matched by his condemnation of anything mean, devious or dishonest in business dealings.

These advantages were counterbalanced by a handicap which would have daunted and probably defeated a man of less resolute character. From the age of six he was a martyr to recurrent and sometimes disabling attacks of asthma. At times, even during important sales weeks, he was forced out of action and into bed. But he always made light of his affliction, and nobody witnessing his confident professionalism on the rostrum would have guessed the cost in courage and nervous energy that his presence demanded. He was veritably a hero of his times.

Sam Watt, the father of Terry, and Gerald Watt, the father of Ken, were two of the five children of Andrew Alexander Watt, who died in 1930. The Watts were a noted family of Northern Irish landowners and sportsmen, and nearly all the members of the family were accomplished horsemen. Andrew Alexander Watt's two daughters, Connie Stern of Hazlegrove House and Eva Holford of Duntish Court, were two of the boldest and most skilful riders with the Blackmore Vale Hounds in the west country of England in the 1920s and 1930s. Gerald, besides being an excellent horseman and polo player, had a fine singing voice and was accompanied regularly by his wife Gladys, who played the piano beautifully. Their combined musical talents formed a considerable social asset in the days before television and sophisticated music centres. Although Ken neither sang nor played a musical instrument, he inherited a keen sense of musical appreciation and was a frequent visitor to Covent Garden for opera and ballet during his years in London while Tattersalls' offices remained at Knightsbridge. His tastes have always been essentially classical, not popular. To a friend who suggested that the Beatles had written some melodies that would endure he retorted sharply: 'I think Liszt wrote some better ones.'

When it was time for Ken to go to his public school he was sent from the family home Drumlerry, at Shantallow in County Londonderry, to Malvern College in the hope that its high altitude in the Malvern Hills would alleviate the symptoms of his asthma. Those hopes were disappointed, because he suffered from the complaint throughout his time at Malvern. However, he passed into Sandhurst and, to his great joy, also passed the medical test. He was remarkably fit throughout the first term there despite all the rigorous drilling under Guards sergeants, and passed triumphantly off the square at the end of the term. But his second term brought a relapse. The asthma returned in more severe form than ever before, and he was so breathless in the mornings that he could not go on parade and was compelled to report sick. Inevitably he was given an adverse medical report and invalided out of the army.

Not for the last time in his life, Ken refused to accept a setback as final defeat. At once he adopted the alternative of army entry through the university, passed the entrance exam and was accepted by Trinity College, Cambridge. He read history for two years and military studies for one year, but he did not allow work to interfere with a full programme of sporting activities. Throughout the winters at Cambridge he kept two hunters in the Fitzwilliam country, and played polo and shot in Norfolk during the appropriate seasons. However, he emerged from his university course with an honours degree, and was duly commissioned in the regiment of his choice, the 15th/19th Hussars.

He went to France with his regiment on the outbreak of the Second World War, but contracted pneumonia during the appalling winter of 1939-40. He was sent into hospital at La Baule, on the estuary of the Loire where, with no antibiotics then available for treatment, he hovered for some days between life and death. Eventually he turned the corner and, when fit enough to travel, was sent back to England, thus avoiding the ordeal of the Dunkirk evacuation.

Ken's next position was as adjutant at the Small Arms School at Netheravon. He enjoyed the work there and felt that he was doing a useful job; he was bitterly disappointed when he was taken from it and posted to what seemed the dead-end job of commanding the cavalry squadron of Cambridge University OTC. However, it did serve the purpose of keeping him in touch with his regiment, because one of his duties was to seek out and report on suitable officer material for the regular cavalry regiments.

Nevertheless if Ken could not go to the war, the war did come to him. One night while he was asleep in his Cambridge lodgings a lone German raider, having been intercepted by night fighters on the approach to its target in the Midlands, jettisoned its load over the city and a 200-kg bomb crashed through the side of the house, fracturing a gas main and setting it ablaze. Miraculously unhurt, Ken awoke to find a gaping hole in the wall of his room, and had to plunge out through the flames onto a pile of rubble in the street outside. His kit and possessions left in the house were destroyed.

In the circumstances, with no hope of being declared fit enough to rejoin his regiment, Ken was bound to find the offer from Tattersalls attractive. However, at first he demurred on the grounds that, despite his wide experience of horses and hunting, his knowledge of thoroughbreds was inadequate. Further consideration induced a change of mind. Many years later he expressed his reasons in words which threw a revealing light on his character: 'I felt that I had let everybody down as a soldier, and that I should take the opportunity to try and make a success of something else.'

Ken's acceptance carried the condition that he would receive no salary for the first year, so that he would be under no obligation if he did not like the work or was unable to get on with other members of the firm. He was able to take this line because he had a private income which made him financially independent. His first impressions were not wholly encouraging. He encountered a certain aloofness, if not outright hostility, from Bob Needham, whose tough Australian upbringing had left him with a prejudice against anyone who had begun life with privileges, like a public school education, which he himself had not enjoyed. Ken was thoroughly disconcerted at his first sales, which he attended still in uniform, by Bob's gruff instruction: 'I'm putting you on to sell twenty lots tomorrow.' Ken was horrified, being only too conscious of his inexperience, lack of familiarity with the techniques of auctioneering and lack of knowledge of the horses he was expected to sell. 'I just had to put the best face on it I could, and I muddled through somehow', he said later.

Not content with throwing him in at the deep end, Bob made a practice of standing behind him during his early sales sessions and uttering a stream of criticisms of his performance in an undertone. On one occasion he kept niggling: 'Get on with it; you're being very slow.' At last Ken lost his temper and, when he had finished selling one lot, drew Bob to the back of the rostrum and told him in a furious whisper: 'Leave me alone; I'm doing my best.' When he had cooled down, Ken felt that he had really burnt his boats, and anxiously awaited a call to Bob's office to be given the sack. At last the summons came, but instead of receiving the sack he heard Bob's conciliatory words: 'I've been thinking it over, and I've decided I was wrong. So now I'd like to shake hands.' From

Kenneth Watt soon after joining the firm

that moment they got on well together.

Ken's association with Tattersalls was formalized in the summer of 1945 when his contract stated that as from 1 July he was engaged as an assistant by Messrs Tattersall in their business as auctioneers and owners of a training establishment, at a salary of £800 a year. By that time he knew Manton well, as he had made a habit of going down there for several days at a stretch in order to go round stables with Joe Lawson and learn as much as he could about horses' legs, infirmities and ailments – much to the astonishment of the trainer, who could not understand why a man of Ken's social standing should want to know about such humdrum matters. He also studied equine conformation under the well-known Oakham veterinary surgeon George Gibson, who imparted to him such pearls of wisdom as his reason for disliking the defect of a horse being 'back at the knees', which was that excessive strain was placed on the back tendons.

The firm was plunged back into management crisis the following summer. Bob Needham had shouldered the burden almost single-handed for many months during the war, and in addition had been kept out night after night on the arduous and often dangerous duties of an air-raid warden. Although he was outwardly as strong and healthy as an ox, the strain must have told. At three o'clock on the morning of 4 June 1947 Ken Watt was woken by the telephone at the Cavalry Club in Piccadilly, where he had a room on permanent let while he was working at Tattersalls' office in Knightsbridge. He answered the call and heard the agitated voice of Mona Needham: 'I am very sorry to tell you that Robert has had a massive heart attack, and has turned over in bed and died.'

Bob's death left Ken in an extreme quandary. Gerald Deane was the sole surviving partner, and he was a broken reed because his volatile temperament had deteriorated to such an extent that he was able to take part in the affairs of the firm only intermittently. He had been in a state of incapacitating depression for months before Bob's death.

Ken's first duty after Bob's death was to travel down to Littleton to inform Gerald. On hearing the news Gerald put his head in his hands and burst into tears. 'We can't go on. We can't go on', he blurted out. Ken assured him that they could and would go on. 'Then you will have to look after everything, my dear boy', Gerald muttered brokenly.

Gerald Deane selling at Newmarket. Kenneth Watt (arms folded) stands on his right

In fact, Gerald's mental health improved during the next few weeks, and Ken was able to persuade him to attend the opening of the First July Sales on the second day of the month, and cajoled him into taking his place on the rostrum. As the starting time approached he broke out in a profuse nervous sweat, and Ken feared that his nerve would crack. But he made a great effort to pull himself together, began by delivering a warm tribute to Bob Needham's memory, and then proceeded to sell his appointed batch of horses, a collection of moderate horses-in-training, with growing self-assurance. The immediate crisis was over.

There were indeed solid grounds for optimism, because signs of a post-war boom in thoroughbreds were manifesting themselves, and foreigners were returning to the market to replenish their bloodstock resources. But if Gerald was able to summon up courage to appear at the sales and go through the motions of auctioneering, his health was in terminal decline. His signature on documents in the summer of 1947 was the shaky scrawl of a very old or sick man, and his actions during those months bore all the marks of indecision, of defeatism even. He refused to authorize any expenditure on refurbishing or modernizing the amenities of the Park Paddocks; Manton was sold in order to raise money to pay Bob Needham's death duties; and the Knightsbridge premises, which had been damaged by a flying bomb in August 1944, were sold to the furniture firm Oetzmann with a lease-back agreement for Tattersalls to occupy offices in the new block to be built on the site. Ken argued strenuously against the Knightsbridge sale, because money could easily have been raised from the banks on the security of such a potentially valuable site, but he had no powers and Gerald would not listen.

It might all have been so different if completion could have been postponed until after 17 December 1947, the date on which Ken Watt became a partner in Tattersalls. Gerald had been the sole owner of Tattersalls since the death of Bob Needham, and the new partnership, which was to run for ten years, was backdated to 1 July 1946. The original capital was to amount to £80,000 with £60,000 contributed by Gerald and £20,000 by Ken, and the profits were to be divided on the basis of two-thirds to Gerald and one-third to Ken. Each partner agreed to have no other business interests, but Gerald was to be at liberty to carry on his stud farm at Littleton, and Ken his estate and farm at Burnley Hall, Somerton, in Norfolk.

The partnership agreement contained one significant clause which had not been included in any of the previous Tattersalls agreements. It stated:

> If and during such period as the health business capacity or discretion of one of the Partners shall become and be so impaired as to make it desirable in the best interests of the Partnership business that he should refrain from taking an active part in the conduct of such business such Partner (in this Clause called 'the non-acting Partner') will if he shall have been requested in writing by the other Partner (in this Clause called 'the acting Partner') so to do refrain from taking an active part in the conduct of the said business except to such extent and in such manner as may be requested or approved by the acting Partner and the conduct of the Partnership business and all things in connection therewith shall be vested solely in the acting Partner. . . .

The inclusion of this clause reflected the delicate state of Gerald's mental health, and there is no doubt that the financial position of Tattersalls as the firm faced the difficult problems of post-war reorganization would have been immeasurably stronger if the partnership, with the protective clause, had been formed 6 months earlier.

It was clear that Ken would soon be left with the main responsibility for the survival of Tattersalls in a formal as well as a practical sense. However, two months before Gerald Deane's death on 17 June 1951 a step to spread the load had been taken with the admission of a new partner, John Coventry. The contract, dated 1 April, established a partnership between Gerald Deane, Ken Watt and the Honourable John Bonynge Coventry, with capital of £70,000 as to £40,000 from Deane, £25,000 from Watt and £5,000 in cash from Coventry. The death of Gerald Deane left Ken Watt, at the age of thirty-seven, as the senior partner.

John Coventry had a pedigree steeped in the best traditions of the Turf. His father, Viscount Deerhurst, was the elder son of the 9th Earl of Coventry who, for years before his death in 1930 at the age of ninety-two, had been revered as the Grand Old Man of British racing. Lord Coventry had won the Grand National in the 1860s with the sisters Emblem and Emblematic and, from the middle of the nineteenth century had tended and improved an obscure non-thoroughbred family so diligently that at last he bred from it the high-class filly Verdict, who won the Cambridgeshire in 1923 and the following year the Coronation Cup, then the most important race in the Calendar for older horses over 1½ miles. Thirty years later Verdict's great-granddaughter Lavant was to strike an epoch-making blow for the untouchables of the racehorse population by gaining admission to Volume 36 of the General Stud Book.

John Coventry also was related to the brothers Captain Henry (Bee) and Arthur Coventry, grandsons of the 8th Earl. Bee Coventry won the 1865 Grand National on Alcibiade but Arthur Coventry, though failing on his five Grand National mounts, was the better jockey. Arthur rode Bellringer to victory in the National Hunt Chase, then run at Derby, in 1879, but excelled as a rider on the Flat. In those days amateurs were permitted to, and often did, ride against professionals on the Flat, and Fred Archer regarded Arthur Coventry as the equal of the best professionals over a mile; while George Lambton, no mean race-rider himself, described him as 'the best amateur I ever saw'.

On retiring from race-riding Arthur Coventry was appointed Jockey Club starter, and achieved as much distinction in that role as he had in the saddle. John Coventry followed in his footsteps when he was appointed starter under the Rules of Racing and National Hunt Rules in 1937. Educated at Eton and Oxford and later commissioned in the Grenadier Guards, he was a first-class cricketer and captained Worcestershire. Tall, fair and upright in stance, he was the physical ideal of the cricketing English gentleman, and was a man of considerable public spirit as he was Mayor of Worcester in 1929 and a JP. He joined Tattersalls after war service with the Airborne Division. Unfortunately he was less assertive on the rostrum than he had been at the crease. He was an indifferent auctioneer, as he had a weak voice and a diffident and sometimes petulant manner. He seldom conveyed the impression that he was on top of the bowling and, like the prune in the old comic song, he had a worried look.

Nevertheless it would be easy to underestimate John Coventry's contribution to the progress of Tattersalls. Everyone – whether buyer or vendor or journalist or groom or ordinary member of the public – appreciated his courtesy and helpfulness. He created an aura of goodwill. Moreover he

John Coventry on the rostrum at the Park Paddocks

applied himself assiduously to the interests of Tattersalls, continuing much of the statistical work originally undertaken by Bob Needham. The international aspects of the December Sales were of particular concern to him, and he was able to come forward with an analysis of the foreign purchases country by country within days of the conclusion of the Sales.

Most importantly, he had excellent American contacts through his half-American mother at a period when the American market was becoming an increasingly lucrative outlet for British thoroughbreds, and he certainly played a big part in the development of this side of the business. Consequently his sudden death at the age of sixty-six in July 1969 was yet another serious setback for Tattersalls in the field of management. Apart from his contribution to the progress of the firm in other respects, he had helped to tide over an awkward period in which the difficulties of the firm were aggravated by the long illness and death of one of the most valued employees, Jack Cherry. Cherry joined the firm at the age of eighteen in 1926 after training in accountancy. He was employed at first in the accounts department, but was soon

From left to right: Gerald Deane, Kenneth Watt, the Park Paddocks manager Mr Charlton, Mrs Gerald Deane and John Cherry in the late 1940s

moved to the bloodstock department, in which he remained until 1939. At the outbreak of war he joined the RAF, and served as an air photographer until he was demobbed in 1945. He had already made his debut as an auctioneer when on leave at the Newmarket First July Sales in 1943, and had won the approbation of no less exacting a critic than Ernest Coussell, the senior partner of the British Bloodstock Agency – 'his maiden effort, and a most successful one', wrote Coussell.

On returning to full-time work at Tattersalls after the war, Cherry became chief bloodstock clerk and also a regular staff auctioneer. He quickly became an expert auctioneer, but developed an illness in 1950 from which he had seemed to be making a slow recovery before his death following an operation four years later. His obituary in the *Bloodstock Breeders Review* contained this tribute:

> He will be remembered particularly for the charm and tact which characterised his dealings with both vendors and purchasers, contacts which made a valued contribution to the happy relationship which Messrs Tattersalls maintain with their clients. He also made many friends among owners and breeders in Ireland, a country he visited occasionally on behalf of the firm.

The loss of Jack Cherry could not fail to have an impact on the efficient operation of the firm, but the death of John Coventry had greater significance in the context of the history of Tattersalls because it marked the end of an era – an era in which Ken had always been the junior partner in years, though he had shouldered the full burden of responsibility long before he became senior partner in a formal sense. Before John Coventry died a new generation of partners – or directors as they had been since the structure of the firm was changed to a private limited company for tax reasons in March 1964 – had come on the scene. They were Terry Watt's son Michael and Gerald Deane's son Bruce, both nearly twenty years younger than Ken. From 1969 until he stepped down from the chairmanship in favour of his first cousin once removed (Michael Watt) at the end of 1982, Ken was presiding over a team that was not only more youthful but more imaginative and forward-looking than his elderly colleagues of the earlier days.

Ken Watt began to collect sporting pictures before the Second World War. The pride of his collection at his home Dingle Stone House at Dunwich, on a lonely, wild and beautiful stretch of the Suffolk coast, is Sawrey Gilpin's immense and magnificent portrait of Colonel Thornton's chestnut stallion Jupiter, which was first exhibited at the Royal Academy in 1792. By Eclipse out of a Tartar mare, Jupiter was bred by Eclipse's owner Dennis O'Kelly and won good races for him over 1 mile at Lewes and Newmarket before joining his sire at stud at Epsom. Later he was moved to Yorkshire, where he lived to the great age of twenty-eight. His picture gains additional interest from the portrayal of a trotting carthorse stallion in the background. Other prized possessions of Ken Watt include pictures of The Baron by Herring and of The Baron's famous son, 'The Emperor of Stallions' Stockwell, by Harry Hall.

This combination of aesthetic appreciation and reverence for the history of the Turf forged in Ken a deep emotional attachment to 'The Fox', which had been a feature of Tattersalls' London auction yard since the 1780s. 'The Fox' sits, with one forepaw raised, on a tall fluted plinth decorated with a motif of dolphins; and is lodged under a stone cupola supported by four columns with Ionic capitals and surmounted by a bust of George IV. Oral tradition is equivocal on the question whether the second Richard Tattersall, with an eye to business promotion, sought the royal permission to add the bust in the 1820s, or the king himself, in his vanity, requested it. In any case, the composition symbolized both the royal connection and the links of Tattersalls with foxhunting, for in the early days hunters and hounds, rather than racehorses, were the staples of the firm's trade.

'The Fox' belonged later at Knightsbridge Green while the hunter sales continued there, with the highlights on the Mondays of Derby and Ascot weeks when all fashionable London seemed to congregate there. Roger Mortimer gave a vivid description of the scene on those occasions in a Tattersalls brochure published in 1976:

> Those Knightsbridge sales brought a refreshing touch of the countryside into London . . . when well-known studs of hunters were dispersed. The covered yard would be filled with individuals

The Fox and its cupola in position at Tattersalls, Knightsbridge

the cut of whose clothes, whether they were Masters of Fox hounds, dealers or out-of-work grooms, hinted strongly of their connection with horses. There was no lack, too, of somewhat formidable ladies, the badges of cavalry regiments firmly pinned in their sensible hats, who clearly were more interested in standing martingales than haute couture.

The ladies, in fact, had been a feature of the Knightsbridge sales scene. In an earlier and more elegant age they had perched on the outside seats of coaches, or thronged the arcaded balcony, to get a better view of the proceedings. The closure of those sales robbed 'The Fox' of its purpose and significance in that location, and soon after he joined the firm Ken conceived the idea of transferring it to Newmarket, where it would be safe from German bombs. Before long he approached Sir Albert Richardson, the leading expert on classical and Georgian architecture, a member of the Royal Fine Arts Commission and later to be President of the Royal Academy, for an estimate of the feasibility and the cost of moving it to the Park Paddocks. Sir Albert came down to Knightsbridge, walked round 'The Fox' several times, studied it from every angle and examined it closely, without uttering a word. Then he climbed the stairs with Ken to the office, commenting favourably on various clocks, pictures and other objects that they passed on the way, but still remaining silent on the subject of 'The Fox'. Ken became increasingly fearful that his project was going to be dismissed out of hand. But once the office door was shut behind them Sir Albert's manner changed, and he came straight to the point. Seating himself at the desk, he said briskly:

> It will be necessary to cut the cupola into sections to transport it to Newmarket. There is only one man in England who can do the job. He will arrive here with his tools at eight o'clock each morning and will work till midday, when he will go off to a pub for lunch and you will not see him again until the next morning. The whole operation will cost you £700.

Ken, not yet a partner, had to get the expenditure authorized by Bob Needham. When he broached the subject, Bob appeared to require several seconds of concentrated mental effort even to recall the existence of 'The Fox'. When he had grasped the point he frowned and replied in a contemptuous tone: 'Oh, that old thing. We don't want to spend £700 on that. We'll throw it on the rubbish dump.' Ken had to bring all his persuasive powers to bear in order to make him change his mind, and the final permission was grudgingly given.

So 'The Fox', whose previous journey had been the short one from Hyde Park Corner to Knightsbridge Green, was expertly moved and installed as the focal point of the Lower Sale Paddock at Newmarket, where horses due to be sold are led round and keenly inspected by scores of prospective buyers. The vast majority of members of the international racing and breeding community who frequent the Park Paddocks at sales times have never known, and could not imagine, the place without its presence.

The installation of 'The Fox' was only the first step towards the realization of Ken's vision of an embellished and fully modernized Park Paddocks worthy of the greatest European bloodstock auctioneering house. In his undergraduate days at Cambridge he had driven over to Newmarket one morning to ride out with one of the trainer's strings. Afterwards at breakfast in the Rutland Arms he had seen a notice that the sales were on that day, and decided to go up and have a look for interest's sake. On reaching the Park Paddocks he was shocked to see their run-down and unkempt appearance and the woefully inadequate amenities of a place where Classic winners and breeding stock of the choicest pedigree were bought and sold. The ramshackle scene made a sad contrast with the pre-war Knightsbridge premises, where the great mahogany doors of the yard were polished daily and everything was spick and span. When he joined the firm he made up his mind to rectify this anomaly as quickly as funds, building regulations and the availability of the necessary land permitted. 'It was a kind of dream', he stated in an interview with the American magazine, *The Thoroughbred Record*, in 1984, 'that here must be evolved the finest sales paddocks in the world, worthy of England and worthy of Tattersalls, with every amenity you could need: a decent ring, bars, cloakrooms and lavatories, heat and light. I've been very lucky to see the dream fulfilled in a lifetime.'

One of the most urgent problems was the shortage of boxes at the Park Paddocks, which involved excessive dependence on the goodwill of local trainers and their willingness to rent boxes during the principal sales, particularly the December

The Newmarket December Sales in the 1950s. Two well-known trainers George Beeby (fleece-lined coat) and the portly Sam Hall figure bottom right. Martin Benson (centre foreground) was once a victim of Gerald Deane's temper (see p. 71)

Sales. Permission to build new boxes was unobtainable in the immediate post-war period, but Ken was able to alleviate this problem by purchasing 120 boxes at the sale of equipment of the disused pony racing track at Northolt. 48 enlarged boxes were built from these, with suitable modifications to the doorways in order to accommodate full-sized thoroughbreds instead of the ponies not exceeding 15 hands that had been stabled at Northolt.

The problem was perennial. As the post-war restrictions were relaxed more boxes were built in the Somerville Paddock to the south and the Wall Boxes area to the east of the Park Paddocks, but the tendency was always for the volume of business, and therefore the number of horses needing to be stabled, to outstrip the building programme. The building of the new sale ring, though essential to the grand design, actually involved a step back in this respect, because fifty boxes in the Upper Sale Paddock had to be demolished to make room for it.

A condition of any solution to the problem, even a temporary or partial solution, was the acquisition of more land. The key was the Solario Stud, comprising 20 acres, adjoining the Park Paddocks on the southern and south-eastern sides and extending as far as the Woodditton road. Tattersalls negotiated unsuccessfully to buy 3 acres of the stud for £6500 in 1963 and 1964, and in 1965 made a formal offer of £40,000 for the whole stud, which was refused. Matters came to a head in 1971 when the stud-owner Peter Larkin was anxious to sell and move to the south coast. Tattersalls were not the only possible buyers in the market. Two leading French breeders were interested in buying it to set up a small racing establishment and build a house for use during the sales, and a Newmarket bloodstock agent was keen to buy part of the property. The negotiations were protracted, and were still not completed when Ken departed for a long-arranged salmon fishing holiday. While he was in the wilds of Iceland a telegram from Michael Watt was delivered to him. It read: 'Bought Solario £91,000. All well.'

The price of £4,550 per acre was steep, being more than three times the price ever paid for stud land in Newmarket up to that time. Moreover the cost of the land represented only a fraction of the total cost of developing the site to meet Tattersalls' needs. Three bridges had to be built across a stream that

The arch, which was moved from Knightsbridge to the Park Paddocks, now dominates the car park

bisected the property. Walkways had to be laid down, and extensive waterworks undertaken. Lavatories, canteens, bars, control offices, tack rooms and unloading bays had to be built. All these works were necessary concomitants of the incorporation of the old Solario yard, with 30 boxes, and the new Highflyer Paddock with 212 (later increased to 240) boxes into the Park Paddocks complex. The initial box-building programme alone cost £137,000, for the boxes were built to the highest specifications and were constructed of Canadian cedar wood, double-skinned and roofed in cedar-wood shingles.

In 1985 there were 685 boxes in the Park Paddocks complex, but these were still insufficient. It would, of course, be uneconomic to provide enough boxes to accommodate every horse catalogued during the biggest sales, which extend over a large number of days. For example, the December Sales of 1985 covered ten days and no single horse among the 2174 catalogued needed to occupy a box for the whole of that period. Nevertheless some of the boxes had to be quadruple-booked and called for the most arduous feats of organization by the office manager Alan Taylor, who commented afterwards that he could have done with another fifty boxes.

The equine and the human are equally important ingredients in a bloodstock sale. If the problem of accommodating the horses was primarily one of quantity, the problem of providing adequate amenities for the men and women, buyers and sellers, who attended the Newmarket sales involved questions of quality as well as quantity. The sale ring which had done duty for decades and was still in use after the Second World War was wooden, draughty, inadequate in size and largely exposed to the elements, which include the bitter east winds which blow straight from the Urals and strike the Park Paddocks, on their eminence above the town of Newmarket, with full force in late November and early December. Speaking of the sale ring conditions in those days, Ken said in the *Thoroughbred Record* interview: 'It was really primitive. When it rained you couldn't keep your catalogue dry, and your notes were wiped out.' Evidently little had changed since 1930. In that year the Italian Marchese Mario Incisa, who was shortly to become a partner in the breeding and racing empire of Federico Tesio, visited the December Sales for the first time and gave this disenchanted description of the Park Paddocks scene in his book *The Tesios As I Knew Them*:*

> How different it was from the centrally-heated and upholstered environment where Tattersalls hold their sales today! A flimsy roof afforded less than adequate protection from the arctic conditions to clients and spectators alike. A bed of straw protected our feet. Only a select few (I never knew how they came to be selected) sat in the comparative warmth of a box-like construction at the foot of the auctioneer's rostrum. In the bitter cold the assembled experts and enthusiasts presented a strange sight to our inexperienced eyes. Their clothes were the most curious assortment of greasy collared mackintoshes, ancient sheepskin jackets, antediluvian overcoats – dirty and worn, fur hats, felt hats with woollen scarves tied over or underneath them, hobnailed boots, hunting boots, wellingtons, fur boots, moth-eaten woollen gloves. In their search for protection from the biting weather the gathering resembled a tramps' convention rather than the elite of the racing world enjoying one of the highlights of the year.

However, the modernization of the Park Paddocks could proceed only by stages, and Ken placed the first priority on the provision of a proper dining room. He argued that you could

** The Tesios as I Knew Them*, by Mario Incisa (J. A. Allen & Co., 1979).

The Pegasus wind-vane surmounting the Park Paddocks sale ring

not expect buyers to come from all over the world and pay high prices for the best British bloodstock unless they could sit down to a good meal in warm and attractive surroundings in which they could have discussions with their friends, associates and professional advisers. The dining room, which was a copy of a Georgian orangery, was built in 1954. Its elegant interior was presided over by Beach's portrait of the founder of the firm and the whole building, which also included a bar, was well received by both the main categories of critics – those who were concerned solely with comfort and convenience and those who were more inclined to judge it from an aesthetic standpoint. The truest of sayings is that you cannot please everyone, and one female client of Tattersalls demanded scornfully of Ken: 'Why did you build a church?' George Blackwell expressed the more widely held view when he wrote in the *Bloodstock Breeders Review*:

The restaurant . . . is of the most pleasing design, harmonising completely with its surroundings and providing food and drink comparable with some of London's best-known establishments. The bar, ante-room and adjacent offices, with their unique and well-preserved relics of Tattersalls two former establishments in London, completed a whole of great charm, dignity and historic interest. It is a place that visitors from all over the world will admire and enjoy . . .

The major project was the new sale ring, and in this instance Ken was determined to achieve an edifice which would be perfectly attuned to its function of selling horses and at the same time a monument to the excellence of the British thoroughbred and the eminence of Tattersalls in the world of the thoroughbred. It must blend with the orangery dining room and be the focal point of the entire complex. The man he turned to without hesitation to undertake the design of the building was Sir Albert Richardson. He was already acquainted with Sir Albert through the episode of 'The Fox', and deeply admired some of his work – notably the graceful Jockey Club building at Newmarket erected in 1934 and the new picture gallery at Anglesey Abbey, where he was a frequent guest of Lord Fairhaven for shooting weekends. Sir Albert accepted with enthusiasm the invitation to design the new sale ring.

Enthusiasm, indeed, was one of Sir Albert's salient characteristics, whether he was teaching at the Bartlett School of Architecture, tracing the progress of the classical tradition from the Palladian movement to the mid-Victorian period, or immersing himself in practical work which included the post-war restoration of St James's Church, Piccadilly. His concept of the building fitting to the Park Paddocks was grandiose, and he gave free rein to his ideas at lunch-time conferences with the Tattersalls partners in a private room at the Normandy Hotel, just opposite the Knightsbridge office, where the standards of food and drink were sumptuous. After lunch he would produce sketches and unfold his plans, with the wonderful flow of talk that had captivated thousands of his students, describing the features of a design that should rival St Peter's, while he should play the role of a latter-day Michelangelo.

Ken Watt himself wrote in Tattersalls' bicentenary brochure that Sir Albert's first water-colour sketch of the proposed new sale ring made Versailles pale into insignificance, and added

The wrought-iron entrance gates at the Park Paddocks

that 'unfortunately this magnificent conception also required a treasury on the lines of the Roi Soleil'. The Tattersalls partners had to tug him gently but firmly back to earth from his soaring flights of fancy, and convince him that there were certain financial constraints. Sir Albert wanted to build in Portland stone, the material from which the cupola of 'The Fox' was hewn; but Portland stone would have been much too expensive, and moulded artificial stone had to be substituted. Sir Albert had plans for a roof adorned with classical statues, but again the cost would have been prohibitive. As each of his more extravagant suggestions was turned down he reacted by throwing his hands in the air and saying that he could not carry on, but he quickly calmed down and accepted the frustrations with good grace.

It is fair to argue that classical statuary would have been inappropriate, absurd even, in the setting of the Park Paddocks. Its absence would have been approved by Dr Johnson, who condemned ornamental architecture on principle, 'because it consumes labour disproportionate to its utility' – even if he was carrying the pragmatic to excessive lengths when he added: 'A fellow will hack half a year at a block of marble to make something in stone that hardly resembles a man. The value of statuary is owing to its difficulty. You would not value the finest head cut upon a carrot.' Boswell commented acidly: 'Here he seems to be strangely deficient in taste.'

Nonetheless, if Johnson was guilty of philistinism in his abrupt condemnation of ornamental architecture in general, his view was surely right in the context of the Park Paddocks and its highly functional sales pavilion. The new ring which finally emerged from Sir Albert's designs was a totally enclosed octagonal building constructed of steel and concrete and faced with bricks and stone under a copper roof surmounted by a lantern and wind-vane in the form of a gilt copper flying horse, dating from the 1780s. The material which gave the most pleasing impression was the specially made 2-inch (as compared with the normal 2½-inch) bricks of mellow red set in recessed mortar. Each of the pair of massive teak doors through which the horses entered and left the ring weighed a ton and was automatically controlled. The interior held an oval parade ring, large enough for horses to extend and show themselves properly at a walk, surrounded by tiers of seats and standing room to accommodate a total of 1000 people. The rostrum area had plenty of room for spotters and auctioneers awaiting their turn to sell, and was flanked on one side by a spacious enclosure for the Press. There was a platform above the rostrum for all the essential electronic equipment and two galleries on which art exhibitions are held

The show must go on. Selling continues in the old sales ring while the frame of the new ring rises in the background

during the main sales; and at ground level the circumference was occupied by a large bar and a series of tiny offices to serve the immediate ringside needs of the principal bloodstock agencies. Free of any superfluous external decoration, the new sale ring stood out beyond challenge as the finest in the world.

The actual cost of £175,000 for the completed building was only a fraction of the estimated cost of implementing Sir Albert's more ambitious designs. The Park Paddocks sale ring was Sir Albert's last important work, and it is sad that his death in 1964 prevented him from seeing the finished building, which was opened at the end of the following year. The appearance and the facilities of the building won general acclaim, but there was one dissentient voice. The 6th Earl of Rosebery was one of the leading owner-breeders of the twentieth century, had won the Derby with Blue Peter and Ocean Swell, and had served as President of the Thoroughbred Breeders Association for many years. He was a man of strong character and definite opinions. Shortly before the opening Ken Watt took him on a conducted tour of the building. At the end of it he faced Ken squarely and told him: 'I like all this very much. But you know Watt, you've made one terrible mistake. You've made it much too big.'

Lord Rosebery was not a man to contradict lightly. Ken held his tongue. The contradiction came in the most practical form two years later, when the much publicized sale of Vaguely Noble took place in a building packed to capacity.

But if Richardson's sales pavilion was pleasing in its appearance and dimensions, if its amenities were ultimately satisfactory by the highest possible standards, the opening did reveal one serious flaw. The *Bloodstock Breeders Review* printed the mealy-mouthed complaint: 'Any new venture is always open to criticism, and one would welcome, for instance, an improvement in the acoustics.' Ken Watt was more forthright: 'The acoustics,' he declared, 'were a disaster.' The trouble was that the auctioneer's voice bounced off the copper roof and the concrete floor in a series of reverberations that rendered it often unintelligible and created conditions that were plainly unacceptable for trading in valuable thoroughbreds. Corrective works which involved covering as much of the floor as possible with coconut matting and lining the roof with a 3-inch thickness of echo-absorbing material, were put in hand as soon as possible. The lining process was accompanied by the

The Park Paddocks at a transitional stage. The old sales office ('the railway station') flanked by the orangery dining-room and the new sales ring

installation of 250 small loudspeakers attached to the backs of the seats. After these measures were completed members of the audience thought they were hearing the auctioneer's voice directly from the rostrum, but were really receiving it from the nearest loudspeaker. The remedies were effective. There were no more complaints about the acoustics.

The sales pavilion had been conceived as the centrepiece of an artistic whole of which 'The Fox', the orangery dining room and a new block to incorporate the sales office and a buffet next to the sales ring were integral components. This new block, opened in 1981, was connected to the dining room and echoed the orangery design.

Not that modernization can ever be achieved entirely without offence to the nostalgically inclined. Some regretted the passing of the old 'railway station' and its clock, which provided a popular rendezvous – 'under the clock'. The 'railway station' comprised a glass-fronted corridor with boards on which sales notices were posted, with access to the office and a small sitting room in which auctioneers could rest between selling sessions. Its lack of convenience was extreme. The office contained a single counter 6 feet long, across which all the sales business had to be transacted; the sitting room was the only place available for private interviews, so the resting auctioneers had to be turned out if Geoffrey Hart, the firm's financial and legal adviser, needed to confront an errant or recalcitrant client.

The new two-storey block removed all these shortcomings. Buyers and vendors were able to transact their business in the capacious main office with its long counter manned by Tattersalls staff. The other facilities included, besides the buffet, a drawing room and two floors of offices for international transport companies, which complemented the bloodstock agency offices round the outside of the sales ring. There was also a room for the St John Ambulance Brigade, an office for Weatherbys, with whom all yearlings bought at the sales have to be registered before they can race in Britain, and a room for the operators of the closed-circuit television, which provides a useful service for checking on sales results and racing results, and also for advertising around the sales complex. These improvements were later supplemented by a large-scale extension of the bar behind the dining room, which had tended to become intolerably crowded at lunch-time and in the evening during the main sales, especially in bad weather.

The completion of the office block meant the virtual fulfilment of Ken Watt's vision of a transformed Park

The Park Paddocks (lower centre) before their modern development. The then tree-lined avenue can be seen left and the railway station in the right middleground. The picture was taken by an RAF officer in 1943

The Park Paddocks in 1967. The new sales ring has been built but the extension of stabling facilities to the east has not begun

Paddocks worthy of Tattersalls' traditions and status in the world of the thoroughbred. He retired from the chairmanship at the end of 1982 and handed over to Michael, though he was very far from severing his connection with the firm. In a message published in Tattersalls' first 1983 *American News Letter* and repeated in the annual statistical brochure, Michael stated:

> In taking over from my cousin Kenneth as Chairman of Tattersalls I would like to pay tribute to his immense contribution both to the Firm and to the Bloodstock industry in the past 30 years.
>
> I'm pleased to say that his invaluable advice and experience will still be available to us as he is to remain on the board.
>
> It is largely thanks to his leadership and guidance that the firm has confirmed and enhanced its status as the top European bloodstock sales company.

Privately Michael stresses two aspects of Ken's personality as vital factors in the modern evolution of Tattersalls. One is

The Park Paddocks in the 1980s. The extension of the Park Paddocks complex as far as the Woodditton road (left side of picture) is complete

his strength of character which, more decisively than his skill as an auctioneer, lifted the fortunes of the firm when it was at a low ebb; the other is the unwavering resolution with which he perpetuated Tattersalls' reputation for integrity. Michael's summing-up is surely just, for Ken is unmistakably a man of absolute honour in thought and deed, and quick to condemn dishonesty and corruption wherever he sees them.

Ken possesses an extraordinary inner strength, fortitude and resilience upon which he has been able to draw in many times of stress. He has fought a constant battle against chronic asthma; he had to pilot the firm through the recurrent management crises of the 1940s and 1950s; and he had to bear a deep tragedy in his most intimate personal relationship. In 1946 he married Elisabeth Mary, daughter of Captain Edward Thornton Hodgson of Cowfold, Sussex. They were a devoted couple, and it was a terrible shock when she died suddenly and without warning in September 1976.

They had three homes successively in East Anglia. The first was Burnley Hall at Somerton, close to the Norfolk coast and 6 miles north of Great Yarmouth. It had a fine estate including Martham Broad, a noted haven for wild life. Ken loved the place, but from the time that some of the interior walls of the old hall were pulled down for restoration work his asthmatic condition was aggravated. It became so bad that he could not sleep, and after months without remission it became obvious that he would have to move.

His next home was Boulge Hall near Woodbridge in Suffolk, a house of historic interest because Edward Fitzgerald, the poet and translator of *The Rubaiyat of Omar Khayyam*, had lived there. The final move was to Dingle Stone House. A Regency house constructed in East Anglian flints with a steep pantiled roof, Dingle Stone House is set on a densely wooded spit of land with a reed marsh on one side and water meadows, protected from the North Sea only by a narrow shingle bank, on the other side. Every two years or so the bank is breached by the pressure of high tides backed up by persistent north winds, and the meadows are flooded for weeks on end. This is a part of the coast which has been eroded relentlessly for centuries. Dunwich, now reduced to a hamlet visible across the meadows from Dingle Stone House, was once a thriving sea-port with a cathedral and twenty churches, but most of it disappeared beneath the waves many years ago.

The remote, and in winter sometimes desolate, locality has many consolations for Ken Watt. He is an ardent naturalist and the 450-acre reed marsh, of which he owns half, is the finest reed marsh in England and a sanctuary for many rare birds. It is the best breeding ground in the country for marsh harriers and bearded tits, and a favoured habitat for snipe, avocet, peewit, redshank and bittern.

Another attraction of Dingle is the pheasant shooting on his own and neighbouring estates. A skilled carpenter, he has a well-equipped workshop in an outhouse and does nearly all the work required for the estate, including making and repairing pens for rearing pheasants. Despite his charm and enviable social gifts, as a widower he is a man of extraordinary independence and self-reliance in spirit and action when he can be spared from Tattersalls business. He prefers faraway places untrammelled by congested traffic and throngs of people. Dingle Stone House is not his only refuge. His first sporting love is salmon fishing, and he is happiest when engaged in it either on his own river in Donegal or his annual holiday in Iceland. The rugged wildernesses of that strange and barren island appeal to him as irresistibly as its superb salmon rivers do. Iceland is a country for the brave and the self-sufficient. There are no luxury hotels, other than in Reykjavik, and living for the sporting visitor is often a matter of the bare essentials. On one occasion Ken was caught in an unseasonable blizzard on a rough and unfrequented track crossing a mountain pass from one salmon river to another. His Land Rover bellied in a snow-drift and, with night falling, he was stranded with no protection against the freezing darkness except a bottle of Scotch fortuitously stowed in the back of the car. There was neither a house nor a hut within miles. He had almost resigned himself to the prospect of death from hypothermia when a truck, probably the only one to pass that way within days, came up behind him and hauled him out of the drift.

That kind of adventure was living dangerously for a chronic asthma sufferer. But Ken, from the time he was invalided out of Sandhurst and fought his way back into the army through the university, has always refused to interpret setbacks as defeats. The same indomitable quality enabled him to save Tattersalls in the difficult post-war years, and set the firm on a prosperous course which, for a long time now, has seemed irreversible.

3

Tattersalls Sales since the Second World War

THERE has been evidence of the impact of Tattersalls sales on Classic racing and breeding since the first half of the nineteenth century. In 1837 Lord George Bentinck, afterwards dubbed by Disraeli the 'Lord Paramount' of the Turf, bought the twenty-two-year-old mare Octaviana with her filly foal by Priam for 54 guineas at the sale of Lord Chesterfield's horses at Hyde Park Corner. The foal was Crucifix, the unbeaten winner of twelve races including the 2000 Guineas, the 1000 Guineas and the Oaks, and the dam of the 1848 Derby winner Surplice. In the second half of the century, when commercial breeding operations were founded and proliferated, the Derby winners Caractacus and Hermit were sold as yearlings at the sales conducted by Tattersalls at the Middle Park Stud, and the Derby winner Sainfoin was sold as a yearling at the sales conducted by Tattersalls at the Royal Paddocks at Hampton Court. Memoir, who was to win the Oaks and the St Leger, was sold on the same day at Hampton Court, this being the first time that future winners of the Derby and the Oaks were sold as yearlings on the same day. Three weeks after the Epsom Classic victories of Sainfoin and Memoir, Memoir's sister La Flèche was sold at Hampton Court for 5,500 guineas, then a record price for a yearling. La Flèche improved on her sister's Classic record by winning the 1000 Guineas as well as the Oaks and the St Leger. In addition the sales of the Derby winners Thormanby, Pretender, Doncaster, Galopin, Sefton, Shotover and Merry Hampton had confirmed the unique reputation of Tattersalls as a source of Classic horses by the end of the century.

The period between the two world wars saw a general advance of commercial breeders on the Classic front, as testified by the fact that six of the Derby winners were sold by

Airborne, ridden by Tommy Lowrey, after winning the 1946 Derby. His owner Mr John Ferguson (hand raised) is at right. Airborne was purchased for 3300 guineas at Newmarket in September as a yearling

Tattersalls as yearlings at either Doncaster or Newmarket. They were Papyrus (won in 1923), Manna (1925), Blenheim (1930), April the Fifth (1932), Windsor Lad (1934) and Mid-day Sun (1937). The prices they had realized as yearlings covered practically the entire range from the 6300 guineas of Manna (the second highest yearling price of 1923) to the 200 guineas of April the Fifth. The end of the Second World War was followed by another Tattersalls-sold Derby winner, the 1946 winner Airborne, who had realized 3300 guineas at the Newmarket September Yearling Sales.

Airborne went on to win the St Leger. He was the harbinger of a new era in which high taxation and death duties took a steady toll of the big private studs which were the traditional sources of Classic performers, and the produce of commercial studs played an increasingly prominent part on the Classic stage. Between 1949 and 1984, 38 individual winners of 41 British Classic races were sold by Tattersalls as either foals or yearlings; and although horses bought for high prices at the principal North American yearling sales have bitten deeply

Nimbus, ridden by Charlie Elliott, beats Amour Drake (far side) and Swallow Tail in a close finish for the 1949 Derby. Nimbus was purchased for 5000 guineas at the Newmarket July Sales as a yearling

into the British Classic cake since the late 1960s, horses sold by Tattersalls like To-Agori-Mou, Circus Plume and Commanche Run were still winning British Classic races in the 1980s.

In one year, 1949, horses sold by Tattersalls made a clean sweep of the Classic races, Nimbus winning the 2000 Guineas and the Derby, Musidora the 1000 Guineas and the Oaks, and Ridge Wood the St Leger. Twelve years later four of the five Classic races were won by horses sold by Tattersalls, Sweet Solera winning the 1000 Guineas and the Oaks, Rockavon the 2000 Guineas and Aurelius the St Leger. Four times three of the Classic winners have been horses sold by Tattersalls as foals or yearlings. In 1953 they were Happy Laughter (1000 Guineas), Nearula (2000 Guineas) and Pinza (Derby); in 1964 Pourparler (1000 Guineas), Santa Claus (Derby) and Indiana (St Leger); in 1966 Kashmir II (2000 Guineas), Glad Rags (1000 Guineas) and Sodium (St Leger); and in 1975 Bolkonski (2000 Guineas), Grundy (Derby) and Bruni (St Leger). Tattersalls have sold five future Derby winners during the period, these being Snow Knight (1974) in addition to Nimbus, Pinza, Santa Claus and Grundy.

Pinza, ridden by Sir Gordon Richards, after winning the Derby in 1953. His owner Sir Victor Sassoon (right, with stick) prepares to lead him in, while his trainer Norman Bertie is at far right. Pinza was purchased for 5000 guineas at the Newmarket July Sales as a yearling

In monetary terms by far the largest price realized by any of these Classic winners-to-be was the 98,000 guineas paid by Sir Robin McAlpine for the filly by High Top out of Golden Fez as a foal at the December Sales in 1981. She won the Oaks under the name of Circus Plume three years later. But at the current level of prices this was not an astronomical figure, and Circus Plume was only the third highest priced foal of her year. It is an astonishing fact that it is necessary to go back to 1945, when racing was in the initial stages of emerging from the ravages of the Second World War, to find the Classic winner-to-be that realized that next highest price in monetary terms, and by far the highest price in real terms, taking into account general inflation and the even steeper inflation of bloodstock values of the next 40 years. The horse concerned was the yearling colt by Nearco out of Rosy Legend, a full brother of that year's Derby winner Dante. Submitted at the Newmarket September Sales, he was bid up to 28,000 guineas before he was knocked down to the local trainer Sam Armstrong, acting for the Maharajah of Baroda. The price

Circus Plume (right of two leaders), ridden by Lester Piggott, winning the Oaks in 1984. She was bought by Sir Robin McAlpine for 98,000 guineas as a foal at the Newmarket December Sales in 1981

was then not only easily the highest ever paid for a yearling at auction anywhere in the world, but was the third highest paid for a horse of any age at a sale conducted by Tattersalls: having been exceeded only by the 37,500 guineas paid for the Triple Crown winner Flying Fox as a four-year-old and the 47,000 guineas for the stallion Solario as a ten-year-old. Dante's brother, who was given the name of Sayajirao, justified his record price by winning the St Leger, in which he thrillingly defeated the French horse Arbar by a head. The contemporary claim that his yearling price 'staggered humanity' was perhaps inflated, and it certainly postulated a universal interest in the affairs of the thoroughbred for which there is no evidence whatever. Nevertheless it is impossible not to sympathize with the writer in the *Bloodstock Breeders Review* who doubted 'whether the price will ever be exceeded, even in the United States'. He could not possibly foresee the soaring inflation of bloodstock values that was to come in the 1970s, and was as well on the target as could be fairly expected, because Sayajirao's purchase price stood as the European record for a yearling for 21 years, until Rodrigo II realized 31,000 guineas

The Fox floodlit during the December Sales

Left: *The Park Paddocks scene featuring the sale ring, the Fox, offices and restaurants*

Left: *Richard Tattersall, the founder of the firm*

Below: *Kenneth Watt, the chairman from 1951 to 1982. From the painting by Peter Walbourn*

Left: *Michael Watt, the chairman since 1983, selling at Newmarket*

Left: *The Park Paddocks sale ring and offices from the east*

An aerial view of the Park Paddocks sales complex

Santa Claus, ridden by Scobie Breasley, being led back after winning the Derby in 1964. He was sold by Tattersalls as both foal and yearling, realizing 800 guineas on the former and 1200 guineas on the latter occasion

at the Newmarket September Sales in 1966.

The sale of Sayajirao secured the future of the Friar Ings Stud of the ebullient and pleasure-loving baronet Sir Eric Ohlson, who had retained Dante to race himself, as one of the most successful vendors of yearlings for a decade, though it did not produce any more performers of comparable quality. That particular sale of a horse who fulfilled expectations, however, should not be viewed in isolation but as the most spectacular manifestation of the recovery from the trough of depression into which the bloodstock industry was plunged by the outbreak of the Second World War. The prices of both yearlings and mares were halved between 1938 and 1939. One of the few bright spots on the bloodstock auction front during the first three years of the war was the sale of the late Lord Furness's high-class bloodstock in 1941, which realized 49,005 guineas and included Carpet Slipper, the dam of the 1000 Guineas and Oaks winner Godiva and the Irish Triple Crown winner Windsor Slipper. Carpet Slipper was bought by Mr Joe McGrath, the owner of Windsor Slipper, for 14,000 guineas.

The first positive signs of recovery were seen in 1942 and reflected the improvement in the war situation. That was the year of victory at El Alamein, the allied landings in North Africa and the annihilation of the German 6th Army at Stalingrad. The dispersal sale of the bloodstock belonging to the late shipping magnate Lord Glanely, who had been one of the heaviest investors in high-class thoroughbreds between the wars, gave a fillip to the market and realized a total of 136,570 guineas. But the upturn extended beyond the effects of that special factor and was manifested also in an increased demand for yearlings. The average price realized by yearlings at all Tattersalls sales was 372 guineas, compared with 476 guineas in 1938, which was reasonably satisfactory in view of the facts that no shipping was available for exports and no-one would have been bold enough to predict an early end to the war and a return to a normal racing programme.

The revival continued in 1943, when average yearling prices rose to 554 guineas, well above the pre-war level. There were

Snow Knight, ridden by Brian Taylor, being led into the winner's enclosure by his owner, Mrs Sharon Phillips, after the 1974 Derby. Snow Knight was purchased for 5200 guineas at the Newmarket Houghton Sales as a yearling

Grundy (Pat Eddery up) after winning the King George VI and Queen Elizabeth Diamond Stakes in 1975. He was bought by Dr Carlo Vittadini for 11,000 guineas as a yearling at the Newmarket October Sales

still no shipping facilities for bloodstock, but optimism was in the air and the December Sales brought buying for Australia, New Zealand, the West Indies, Canada, the United States and South American countries for shipping after the war. The overseas purchases included the stallion Felicitation, a great stayer in his racing days, who realized 4500 guineas for export to Brazil. By 1944 the market was in a state of full boom. The aggregate for all Tattersalls sales reached 1,050,457 guineas, the first time it had topped the million mark. The sensitive indicator of yearling prices achieved an advance from 554 to 887 guineas, an increase of more than 60%, in spite of the fact that 116 more lots were on offer than in 1943. The five days of the December Sales, which featured mares, fillies, foals, horses-in-training and stallions, aggregated 517,772 guineas, an all-time record and nearly double the 1943 figure. Carpatica topped the sale at 15,000 guineas, a record for a two-year-old filly. She had won once and been placed second in her other two races, and was allotted 8st. 10lb. in the Free Handicap, so her form was good; but her chief attraction was her superb pedigree, as she was by the dual Classic winner and champion sire Hyperion out of Campanula, who won the 1000 Guineas in 1934. High-class broodmares like Mercy, Sister Clara (destined to be the granddam of the Derby winner Santa Claus) and the 1937 1000 Guineas and Oaks winner Exhibitionist all realized five-figure sums. The export trade was very active, with 50 lots purchased for Argentina alone.

Boom conditions continued unabated in 1945, when the yearling that was to be called Sayajirao was of course the star turn, and the number of horses sold by Tattersalls rose above the 2000 mark, and 1946, when Tattersalls' turnover was 2,156,825 guineas, more than 100% above the 1944 level. A number of factors combined to produce this astonishingly rapid escalation. Foreign demand was very strong, with buyers from the countries of liberated Europe, particularly France, supplementing those from farther afield; the restoration of the normal racing calendar after the severely restricted programme of races permitted in wartime stimulated home demand; early peacetime euphoria accounted for tremendous increases in racecourse attendances and in betting, and affected sentiment in the bloodstock market; and many people with money to spend turned to racing and bloodstock as a result of the shortage of other luxury goods to buy.

Racing was as popular as ever in 1947, when the number of races contested, 2098, was 300 more than the previous year and well in excess of the total of 1985 in 1938, the last full racing season before the war. However, the fuel crisis exacerbated by the appalling winter of 1946–7 and the ensuing economic recession could not fail to impinge on the bloodstock market. The most notable event of the year was the return of Tattersalls' principal yearling sales to the Glasgow Paddocks in Doncaster in St Leger week. This return was marked by the achievement of a world record aggregate for a yearling sale, 597,725 guineas, but market analysts noted that the average price of 1827 guineas was lower than the average realized at the corresponding sales held at Newmarket a year earlier. By the time of the December Sales the levelling-off of the market was unmistakable, and both average and aggregate prices were substantially down on the previous year. The immediate post-war boom was over, and the bloodstock market was on a plateau on which it was to remain for 8 years.

Humphrey Finney, President of the American Fasig-Tipton sales company, and Kenneth Watt, chairman of Tattersalls, prepare to drink a toast at a Newmarket reception

The fact of being on a plateau in respect of prices did not mean that Tatteralls sales were devoid of interest or occasional dramatic incident. The December Sales always presented an extremely animated scene, for they were the great annual rendezvous of the bloodstock representatives of many nations. Americans invariably invaded the Park Paddocks in force at that time, and among them none was a more regular or more welcome visitor than Humphrey S. Finney, known to many of his innumerable friends simply as 'Finney'. The son of a Lancashire parson, he had travelled out to the United States at the age of eighteen in charge of a consignment of horses, had immediately taken a liking to the country and put down his roots there. He rose eventually to be president of the Fasig-Tipton Company, which combined the functions of a leading bloodstock auctioneering house and international bloodstock agents. He also gained wide recognition as an expert in stud management. It was mainly in his capacity of bloodstock agent that he attended the December Sales, and his short, chunky figure, supported on one of his unique collection of walking sticks, with his half-glasses perched precariously on the tip of his nose, was familiar to everyone in the industry: while his ready smile, wisdom, integrity and marvellously warm personality made him one of the best-loved and most trusted members of the international bloodstock community.

On returning from the December sales in 1951 Humphrey Finney described his impressions in an article for the Virginia sporting paper *The Chronicle* which was afterwards reprinted in the *Bloodstock Breeders Review*: He wrote:

The first Monday of December is the traditional opening of the sales, and this year it was a grand day, though quite cold. The December Sales feature breeding stock, foals and race horses, with few yearlings being offered. This year, of 1115 catalogued, only 60 were yearlings. Generally speaking, yearlings offered here are either sold in dispersals or ones which have failed to come up at the various sales devoted to yearlings.

Sales start at 9.15 daily except for the first day when a 15-minute concession is allowed and affairs get under way at 9.30. There is none of the hurly-burly of the average American auction, everything being done with complete restraint and decorum in the true British manner.

Despite the fact that the Fasig-Tipton Company had numerous orders for foals we returned empty handed in this field, having had to bow to the superior weight of Kentucky dollars in the pocketbook of Arthur B. Hancock Jr on two occasions. The sales continue until 7.00 or 7.30 at night without any break whatever. There is no announcer at English sales, the auctioneer handling the business entirely. No fanfare is made, regardless of the quality of the offerings, but enough time is taken to get every guinea available for the horse.

At Newmarket, such seating as is available is arranged in three tiers in a circular enclosure. The seats themselves are covered, though the horses are open to the elements overhead and are walked or ridden around and around a straw ring. They are not stood for inspection while being sold, as is the case here.

The custom of bidding against a reserve is unfamiliar to most Americans, though it is an entirely fair and practical plan. All bidding must be done through the auctioneer, who will carry the horse up to the last bid, and, if not sold, simply drops the hammer without comment. If the horse is sold he will either mention the buyer by name or will refer to him as 'the gentleman in the gate' or in some similar fashion.

Prince Aly Khan in earnest conversation with Humphrey Finney at the Park Paddocks

Finney's article gave a vivid impression of the December Sales scene and Tattersalls' procedures as seen through the eyes of an intelligent foreigner in the same trade. Arthur Boyd Hancock, to whom he made reference, became better known as 'Bull' Hancock and the owner of one of the world's most famous studs, Claiborne in Kentucky. He led the way among American breeders who were seeking fresh blood, practically regardless of expense, all over the world, and his more sensational purchases included the stallion Nasrullah, who was destined to have a profound impact on thoroughbred evolution while stationed at Claiborne. His purchases at the 1951 December Sales were in a lower financial key, for he bought the two filly foals mentioned by Finney and four mares for a total of 21,700 guineas. Nevertheless two of the mares were to prove bargains of a rare order. Within the space of 24 hours he bought the seven-year-old Rough Shod, in foal to My Babu, for 3500 guineas, and the ten-year-old Knight's Daughter, in foal to Watling Street, for 2500 guineas. Each of these mares was to have a dramatically beneficial impact on the fortunes of Claiborne and, indeed, on the quality of American breeding as a whole. Rough Shod, or Rough Shod II as she was called in the United States, bred the champion filly Moccasin and other top-class horses including Ridan and Lt. Stevens as a result of matings with Nasrullah's son Nantallah, and founded a family which produced scores of good horses including Thatch and Nureyev; and Knight's Daughter bred the outstandingly tough and brilliant Round Table, who as a stallion was a perfect foil to the influence of the more volatile Nasrullah.

Rough Shod and Knight's Daughter were members of leading British thoroughbred families and were supreme examples of the flair of perspicacious buyers for skimming off the cream of the bloodstock market from time to time without paying top prices.

The December Sales of 1951 realized a total 100,000 guineas higher than the previous year, but Finney attributed the somewhat flat tone of the proceedings to the lack of any important dispersals. Dispersals of the bloodstock of people who have raced or bred thoroughbreds on a large scale have always stimulated the interest of buyers and two years earlier the dispersal of the horses-in-training of Lord Portal, who had died in April, realized 70,850 guineas for fourteen lots at Tattersalls First July Sales. They included the two-year-old filly Red Ray, for whom the bidding rose to 12,000 guineas, the second highest price of the consignment, before she was knocked down to the American trainer James Ryan. It was a momentous purchase. Ryan bought Red Ray for Paul Mellon, whose Rokeby Farm in Virginia was one of the most select of American private studs. She bred only two foals, but one of them was Virginia Water, who was not only a top-class performer, winning the two-year-old fillies championship race, the Cheveley Park Stakes, and finishing second in the 1000 Guineas and the Oaks, but earned greater fame as the granddam of Mill Reef. Mill Reef was one of the most brilliant Derby winners of the second half of the twentieth century when he scorched home at Epsom in 1971, and afterwards became a top-ranking Classic stallion at the British National Stud; but none of this would ever have happened if Jim Ryan, having reached Mellon's stated limit of 10,000 guineas on that July evening in 1949, had not been persuaded by his English pressman friend, Clive Graham, to go on bidding.

A greater dispersal was largely responsible for a giant leap forward of the bloodstock market in 1954, when the total of

2,386,476 guineas for all Tattersalls sales easily surpassed the record which had stood since 1946, and the totals for yearlings at all Tattersalls sales and for the December sales both exceeded a million guineas for the first time. The dispersal was that of the bloodstock of the whisky magnate James A. Dewar, who had died in August, at the December Sales. As George Blackwell commented in the *Bloodstock Breeders Review*, the Dewar horses attracted such frenzied bidding that 'prices soared until by the end of the week all preconceived ideas of values had become anachronisms'.

Dewar had accumulated one of the choicest collections of mares in England at his Homestall Stud in Sussex, and had bred such Classic horses as the 2000 Guineas and Derby winner Cameronian, the Oaks winner Commotion and the brilliant Tudor Minstrel, who won the 2000 Guineas in 1947 by a margin of no less than 8 lengths, though he afterwards caused one of the biggest betting upsets in the history of the Derby when he failed to stay at Epsom. Brochures containing details of all the bloodstock had been prepared and sent to likely buyers all over the world, arousing widespread interest. As it had been estimated that 40% of the total sum realized at the Doncaster yearling sales had been attributable to overseas buyers, and American breeders, who enjoyed a favourable rate of exchange, were present in force at the Park Paddocks in December, it was confidently predicted that most of the Dewar mares would be crossing the Atlantic. This outcome was anticipated gloomily by many breeding pundits, who had been lamenting the drain on British thoroughbred resources as a result of excessive exports for some time. Ken Watt referred to this in an announcement from the rostrum before he sold the main batch of Dewar mares on Tuesday morning:

> As it is my somewhat melancholy duty to offer these horses, I should like to pay tribute to the great debt owed by the Bloodstock Industry to those private breeders like Mr Dewar, who have done so much to foster and preserve the best lines of blood in this country and in Ireland. Now that the immense scale of death duties has dictated the break-up of this wonderful collection of mares, is it too much to hope that at least some of them may remain in the British Isles?

To the general surprise and delight, the answer to his

Two famous trainers, Sir Cecil Boyd-Rochfort and Atty Persse, discuss the catalogue. They both lived to over ninety

question was in the negative: no, it was not too much. The first lot from this batch was the nine-year-old Nearco mare Phaetonia, who had shown first-class speed to win the Molecomb Stakes at Goodwood. She was knocked down for 15,500 guineas to Cecil Boyd-Rochfort who, it was assumed, was bidding for one of the Americans whose horses he trained; but in fact he was acting on behalf of the Someries Stud of his English clients Sir Harold and Lady Zia Wernher. Phaetonia's colt foal by Alycidon was bought by the American trainer Jim Ryan for 8000 guineas, and others among the less highly valued Dewar lots were bought by American interests. But when the most prized Dewar mares came into the ring British buyers were in the ascendant. Dr John Burkhardt bought Minaret, a great-granddaughter of Dewar's wonderful foundation mare Lady Juror, for 22,000 guineas and the five-year-old mare Refreshed, who had won four races and been third in the 1000 Guineas, for 30,000 guineas, making the purchases for Mr J. R. Hindley of the Ribblesdale Stud and Mr Gerald Askew respectively. However, the most spirited bidding of all was reserved for Refreshed's half-sister Festoon, the next lot but one. Festoon had won the 1000 Guineas seven months earlier and, after an opening bid of 25,000 guineas, the bidding resolved itself into a duel between the bloodstock agent David McCall, acting for the American Mrs Elizabeth Graham, and Gerald Askew's brother Tony. At 35,000 guineas the bid was McCall's but, after an appeal by Ken Watt, Askew ventured 1000 guineas more, and that was enough to silence the American challenge. There was an outburst of cheering from the audience when the name of the successful bidder was announced, and it was realized that these two choice mares were to stay in England. The sum of 36,000 guineas paid for Festoon was the third highest ever recorded at auction, having been exceeded only by the 47,000 guineas paid for Solario twenty-two years earlier and by the 37,500 guineas paid for Flying Fox in 1900.

For Refreshed and Festoon the transactions meant moves of only a few miles from Homestall, because the Askew brothers both had studs in Sussex. They were nephews of the flour-milling magnate James A. Rank, who had been a great supporter of both flat and jump racing and had won the 1938 St Leger with Scottish Union, a horse he had bought from the Sledmere Stud for 3000 guineas at Tattersalls Doncaster Yearling Sales.

Rex Ellsworth was one of the Americans present at the Dewar dispersal, though he was not a purchaser. A devout Mormon and a cattle rancher on a vast scale in Arizona and New Mexico, Ellsworth had begun to accumulate thoroughbred breeding stock in the 1930s and emerged as one of the leading American breeders after the Second World War, with a powerful breeding operation in California, where his unorthodox methods caused some raised eyebrows among the traditional breeders of Kentucky. His most important acquisition was Hyperion's son Khaled, who had been second in the 1946 2000 Guineas and sired the Kentucky Derby winner Swaps, only the second California-bred winner of the premier American Classic race, for Ellsworth.

Khaled had been bred and raced by the Aga Khan, so it was hardly surprising that Ellsworth was back at the December Sales in 1957 and taking a close interest in the dispersal of many of the bloodstock of the Aga Khan, who had died that year. This dispersal realized 177,030 guineas for 51 lots, and of these totals Ellsworth accounted for 89,120 guineas and 24 lots. His concentration on the Aga Khan's bloodstock is demonstrated by the fact that he made only five other purchases for a total of 5150 guineas at the same sales.

Ellsworth's 1957 December Sales purchases brought little material advantage to his stud operations. They included the fifteen-year-old Nikellora, winner of two French Classic races and the Prix de l'Arc de Triomphe, for 12,000 guineas and Double Rose III, the dam of the Champion Stakes winner Hafiz II, for 10,500 guineas, but the best bargain was Bodala, who cost only 650 guineas. Bodala became the dam of the Hollywood Oaks winner Delhi Maid, who appropriately was by Khaled. Another bargain was Djenne for 4000 guineas, as she was carrying the good racehorse and stallion Olden Times. Certainly none of these Ellsworth purchases had anything like the impact on American, or for that matter world breeding, of the purchase of Lady Angela at the December Sales in 1952. Submitted by Martin Benson from the Beech House Stud, the Hyperion mare Lady Angela was in foal to Nearco and was bought for 10,500 guineas, the top price of the sale for a broodmare. She was acquired by George Blackwell, who was then on the staff of the BBA, for the Canadian Eddie Taylor. The foal she produced the next year, Empire Day, was disappointing, but she was covered by Nearco again before she was shipped to Canada. This time the produce was Nearctic, who was not only a very good racehorse himself but the sire of Northern Dancer, the world's best Classic sire in the 1970s and 1980s and a great sire of sires.

Although the Americans have been the most consistent and cumulatively far the heaviest spenders, the December Sales have attracted buyers from every continent and every country in which the breeding of thoroughbreds is pursued. The interest of the Japanese has been intermittent, but at times their impact on the market has been very considerable. They returned to England in 1952 for the first time since the Second World War in search of stallions and the following year, besides making a private purchase of the stallion Gay Time, who was second in the 1952 Derby, they invested in 29 in-foal mares. The mares included the twelve-year-old Nearco mare Neandria, for whom they paid 3700 guineas through the BBA. Nine years later several strong Japanese contingents helped to compensate for temporarily diminished interest from the United States. On that occasion their purchases included the highest price of the week, 20,000 guineas for the

The animated scene in the Park Paddocks as horses are paraded before sale

five-year-old mare Paradisea in foal to Charlottesville through the Anglo-Irish Agency.

At some December Sales, when their Government's import controls were relaxed to permit free spending on bloodstock, Japanese buyers, shepherded by their British agents, were prominent in clusters in the Park Paddocks or seated in rows opposite the rostrum in the sales pavilion. In time, however, the groups tended to disappear and Japanese buying was concentrated in the hands of wealthy individual breeders bidding *in absentia* through their agents. One of the most spectacular of these forays occurred in 1978, when the British agent John Corbett, of Heron Bloodstock Services, bought four lots totalling 514,000 guineas for his client Higeto Furuoka. These lots included the four-year-old Royal Hive, winner of the Park Hill Stakes the previous year, for 224,000 guineas. This eclipsed the December Sales record of 154,000 realized by the 1000 Guineas winner Mrs McArdy the previous year, but Royal Hive's price was easily exceeded by the 325,000 guineas realized by the Champion Stakes winner Swiss Maid at the same sales.

In the nineteenth century Tattersalls held sales at many

different places. In 1865, for example, there were important sales at Albert Gate, Newmarket and Doncaster; there were sales of high-class yearlings at the Royal Paddocks at Hampton Court and at William Blenkiron's Middle Park Stud in Kent; there were sales at Reading and Stockbridge racecourses, Ashgill near Middleham, Nelson's stables at York and the Grosvenor Hotel stable-yard at Chester; and there were miscellaneous sales like those of chargers, hunters and hacks at Colchester barracks and hunters and hounds at Abingdon, Banbury and Shrewsbury. From the turn of the century the number of venues and the variety of the lots sold steadily dwindled. After the Second World War Tattersalls traded only in thoroughbreds, and the only important venues were the Glasgow Paddocks at Doncaster and the Park Paddocks at Newmarket, though secondary mixed sales were held at Epsom's Tattenham Corner for a brief period in the late 1950s.

Even the Doncaster Sales had been suspended during the war, when the racecourse and the Glasgow paddocks were commandeered by the Army and became the headquarters of the Royal Army Veterinary Corps. The Doncaster September Sales, held in St Leger week, were traditionally the most important in the yearling market. In 1928, when the blood-stock market between the two world wars reached its peak, 344 yearlings were sold at Doncaster for an average of 996 guineas, compared with 239 for an average of 662 guineas at the Newmarket First and Second July Sales combined and 142 for an average of 418 guineas at the Newmarket October Sales. The ascendancy of Doncaster was confirmed as soon as the Glasgow Paddocks reopened in 1947, for 337 yearlings were sold for an average of 1,827 guineas in St Leger week, while 228 were sold for an average of 782 guineas at the two Newmarket July Sales and 332 were sold for an average of 817 guineas at the Newmarket First October Sales.

A number of famous studs were long-established sellers at Doncaster. Among them was Sledmere, whose product Scottish Union had won the last St Leger run at Doncaster before the war. The sale of the Sledmere yearlings on the Thursday of St Leger week was always an eagerly awaited event and accompanied by a good deal of showmanship, with the yearlings being led up by liveried attendants. The Sled-mere consignment of 1947 did not disappoint the critics, and the seven lots realized a total of 24,570 guineas and an average

Kenneth Watt selling at Doncaster

of 3510 guineas, an average exceeded only by the 3898 guineas for the seven lots from Commander Peter Fitzgerald's Mondellihy Stud among those selling more than three lots. The National Stud, a newcomer to Doncaster, obtained the highest aggregate with 31,630 guineas for 10 lots. Sledmere obtained its top price of 7500 guineas for a colt by Dastur out of Participation. However, the true pearl among the Sledmere yearlings was the colt by Bois Roussel out of Hanging Fall, knocked down to the trainer Noel Murless for 4000 guineas. Two years later this colt won the St Leger under the name of Ridge Wood.

In 1951 the lease of the Glasgow Paddocks was renewed. Doncaster Corporation gave Ken Watt and John Coventry the sole right to use the Paddocks until 1 October 1957 at an annual rent of £1,000, which compared with the previous rents of £550 agreed in 1936 and £400 in 1920. The Corporation was to pay the rates and taxes on the paddocks and was obliged to keep the boxes in good repair.

Doncaster retained its primacy among the yearling sales for the duration of the new lease, in respect both of prices and the quality of the horses sold. Belle of All, winner of the 1000

Guineas in 1951; Happy Laughter and Nearula, winners respectively of the 1000 Guineas and the 2000 Guineas in 1953; and Ballymoss, winner of the St Leger in 1957 and afterwards an eminent Classic sire, all were sold there as yearlings. Nevertheless, it was increasingly apparent that the facilities of the Glasgow Paddocks were woefully inadequate for the premier sales of their kind. The sale ring was pitiful in comparison even with the mediocre standards ruling in the Park Paddocks at the time. The ring itself consisted of a single white circular post and rail fence 2 feet 6 inches high. It was located in a paddock of tufted, unkempt grass, and the horses wore a bare earth track round the inside of it as they were led for the inspection of bidders. The rostrum was in a ramshackle wooden shed. There were no steppings to enable bidders and spectators to get a proper view; the only raised viewing and shelter from the elements was in a stand set 20 yards back from the ring. Although a timber and felt roof had been added at a cost of £1000 in 1930, the stand was primitive and looked as if it might have been obtained second-hand from one of the minor National Hunt meetings. In view of the plans for modernizing and transforming the Park Paddocks, it really did not make sense to prolong the life of the Doncaster St Leger Sales indefinitely, except in so far as they were sanctioned by tradition and the customary trading patterns of buyers and sellers. However, the occasion for the termination of Tattersalls activites in Doncaster was the expiry of the lease in 1957, the Corporation's requirement of the Glasgow Paddocks for civic development and the prohibitive cost of building suitable facilities at another site in the town. In addition there had been a growing number of complaints about the shortage of good hotel accommodation in the area and the inaccessibility of Doncaster to foreign buyers.

For these reasons the final session of Tattersalls' yearling sales at Doncaster was held on the morning of Friday 13 September 1957. At the end of the session Ken Watt announced: 'And that, gentlemen, concludes the sale', and proceeded to read the following prepared statement from the rostrum:

We should like to take this opportunity of expressing the feelings of the firm of Tattersalls during this, the last Doncaster Sales.

We have sold horses in Doncaster since 1828, and the Yearling

Sales have been famous for generations. These are changing times, but it had been hoped that the Sales would continue here at Doncaster on another site. The Corporation of Doncaster and we in Tattersalls have examined this possibility from every aspect. We much regret to say that the project has proved to be an uneconomic one for both parties in these difficult times.

During this final week, we should like to express our deep thanks to the Corporation and to their predecessors for well over a century. In particular we should like to thank the Racecourse Manager and his staff in the Paddocks. We have truly appreciated the aid and the interest shown by the people of Yorkshire, that great home of sport and the British Thoroughbred.

It is with feelings of nostalgia that we leave here, and that an era closes in the history of Doncaster and of Tattersalls.

Although in later years a new sales company, Doncaster Bloodstock Sales Ltd, was formed to operate at Doncaster and traded successfully not only in yearlings but in all categories of thoroughbreds, the supremacy of Tattersalls was never threatened by the decision to concentrate all their selling at Newmarket. The former Doncaster Sales were held in the Park Paddocks on Wednesday and Thursday 3 and 4 September 1958. The fact that there was no racing at Newmarket that week made it possible to compress into two days, with morning and afternoon sessions, sales that had occupied four days at Doncaster, where there had been racing in the afternoons. The leading Yorkshire studs like Sledmere, Burton Agnes, Friar Ings and Theakston, and Irish breeders like Tally Ho Stud, Collinstown Stud and Frank Tuthill, whose consignments had been features of the Doncaster September Yearling Sales, all transferred their business to the Newmarket September Sales without any ill effects. On the contrary, the market at the Newmarket September Yearling Sales in 1958 proved satisfactorily strong. Whereas the last Doncaster September Yearling Sales held by Tattersalls had resulted in the sale of 283 lots for an aggregate of 412,394 guineas and an average of 1457 guineas, the transferred sales in 1958 resulted in the sale of 308 lots for an aggregate of 490,300 guineas and an average of 1592 guineas. Burton Agnes and Sledmere occupied the first two places on aggregate for individual sellers, with Tally Ho, the most successful of the Irish vendors, in third place.

In 1958 other important yearlings-only sales were held at

Newmarket in August and during the First October race week, while smaller numbers of yearlings were sold at the all-category Second October, Houghton and December Sales. The transfer of the former Second July Yearling Sales to August had been made the previous year. The July Sales had been declining steadily in aggregate and average prices, as well as the number of yearlings offered and the percentage sold, throughout the decade. Although there were occasional bright spots in respect of the quality of the yearlings sold, as when the subsequent Derby winner Pinza was bought for 1500 guineas by Sir Victor Sassoon in 1951 and the subsequent 2000 Guineas winner Our Babu was bought for 2700 guineas by Mr David Robinson two years later, the sickness of the July Sales had clearly been terminal as buyers held off, knowing that there would be plenty of opportunities later in the year with consequent reduction in the expense of keeping their purchases until they were ready to run.

After 1958 periodic changes were made in the timing and the format of the main yearling sales in response to trends in the national and international bloodstock markets. In 1960 the August Sales, which had not been popular, were transferred to the Houghton Sales in late October, and in 1964 the September Sales also were shifted to Houghton week. For some years the gap between prices at the September Sales, which traditionally were the most important, and at the October Sales had been steadily decreasing. The conclusion drawn by Tattersalls was that buyers liked to keep their money in their pockets for a few weeks longer, and as vendors at the September Sales included many of their oldest and most respected clients, the change seemed equitable. It also seemed to be effective, because prices at the new Houghton Yearling Sales rose by 8.9% to 2366 guineas, while those at the October Sales a fortnight earlier rose by only 5.2% to 2046 guineas. In 1965 the contrast between the two main yearlings sales was even greater because average prices at the September Sales fell back by 24% in sympathy with a general slump in the bloodstock market, but prices at the Houghton Sales managed a 2% rise in spite of the fact that more yearlings were on offer and the duration of the Sales had been doubled from two to four days. In 1966 the return of more stable market conditions set the stage for a series of bidding duels between the American precious-metals magnate Charles Engelhard and the Englishman David

Catalogue seller at the Park Paddocks with Ernest Linsell

Robinson, who had made a fortune in the radio business. Between them they spent more than 215,000 guineas to buy forty yearlings that year.

Engelhard, whose career as an owner was to reach its climax with the Triple Crown victories of Nijinsky in 1970, bid mainly through his racing manager David McCall. He was one of the biggest spenders in the international bloodstock market, and directed much of his buying effort towards the acquisition of potential Classic horses at the North American Sales. Robinson, on the other hand, confined his attention to the main yearling sales in England and Ireland and, although Meadowville carried his colours into second place behind Nijinsky in the St Leger, concentrated his buying drive on horses bred to have precocious speed. On the Classic scene Our Babu, whose maximum distance was a mile, was much more typical than Meadowville. But horses like So Blessed, Green God and Deep Diver, calculated to excel over short

Lord ('Bill') Harrington, one of the chief buyers for the huge David Robinson stable in the 1960s and 1970s

distances at two years old and afterwards as sprinters, were even more typical of the horses in which he invested than Our Babu.

David Robinson was not merely a lavish spender on yearlings. He set new standards of professionalism in his approach to the problems of yearling-buying by employing a team of experts, including the well-known retired trainer Jack Colling and the prominent Irish breeder Lord Harrington, to inspect, select and value the yearlings on offer before the sales and to bid on his behalf. Their advice was absolutely crucial to the enormous success that he achieved as an owner in the late 1960s and the early 1970s. His methods were afterwards developed, refined and adapted to buying yearlings on an international scale by Robert Sangster, Vincent O'Brien and their associates, though the difference between the Robinson and Sangster operations was more than a matter of scale. Whereas Sangster and his associates sought to buy horses with Classic pedigrees for their potential stallion value, Robinson's aim was to buy horses capable of bringing the quickest possible return on the racecourse.

Robinson's most significant purchase in 1966, the year he and Engelhard so often dominated the scene in the Park Paddocks, was the colt by Princely Gift out of Lavant that was knocked down to Lord Harrington for 8900 guineas at the October Sales. Named So Blessed, he possessed brilliant speed, was unbeaten at two years and won three of the most important sprint races – the July Cup, the King George Stakes and the Nunthorpe Stakes – at three years old. The prowess of So Blessed and his champion sprinter half-sister Lucasland had a revolutionary impact on the General Stud Book by persuading Weatherbys, the owners of the Stud Book, that their dam Lavant, previously excluded as non-thoroughbred, must be admitted, together with her offspring and descendants. Her admission ushered in a new era of liberalism in Stud Book policy.

Lord Harrington made other strikingly successful purchases for Robinson when he bought the colt Red God out of Thetis II for 4300 guineas at the October Sales in 1969 and the colt by Gulf Pearl out of Miss Stephen for 8400 guineas at the Houghton Sales the following year. The former, named Green God, became a top-class sprinter, gaining his most resounding victory in the Vernons Sprint Cup. The latter, named Deep Diver, was even more brilliant; he won seven races in England and France at two years old, breaking the 5-furlongs course record when he won the Prix du Petit Couvert at Longchamp; and at three years old won the Nunthorpe Stakes (afterwards the William Hill Sprint Championship) at York in record time, and the most important French sprint race, the Prix de l'Abbaye at Longchamp.

The examples of So Blessed, Green God and Deep Diver demonstrate that there were horses of superb merit in their own category among those picked by the Robinson team. Others of comparable merit bought for Robinson as foals or yearlings at Tattersalls included Idle Rocks, Tudor Music, Yellow God and Bitty Girl. However, the distinctive characteristic of the Robinson racing empire was its legion of speedy performers, by no means all in or near the top class, who accumulated victories in unprecedented numbers season after season. He was leading owner, in terms of prize money, only once, in 1969, when he won 96 races and £92,553; but in 1970 he won 109 races and three years later 115, an all-time record for the British Turf. The next year he had 90 wins, still a

The leading Irish breeder Mrs Jane Levins-Moore with the Royal stud manager Michael Oswald and Lady Angela Oswald in front of the orangery dining-room

gigantic total in comparison with his rivals, but after that he began to reduce the scale of his operations and the number of victories dwindled. The foundation of the success of the Robinson era of ownership had been intensely selective buying at Tattersalls.

David Robinson was succeeded by the Indian-born shipping and tanker owner Ravi Tikkoo as a lavish spender at the yearling sales. At the Houghton Sales in 1973 he paid the two highest prices of the year for sons of Habitat that came up as successive lots from the Killarkin Stud of Mr and Mrs W. F. Davison. The first of them, a chestnut out of Garvey Girl, cost 72,000 guineas and was named Hot Spark; and the second, a bay colt out of A.1, cost 1000 guineas less and was named Steel Heart. They justified these prices by developing into top-class two-year-olds and sprinters. Hot Spark won the 5-furlongs Flying Childers Stakes at two and the Palace House Stakes over the same distance at three years old, while Steel Heart did even better by winning two of the most important two-year-old races, the Gimcrack Stakes and the Middle Park Stakes, and the Duke of York Stakes and Germany's international sprint race, the Goldene Peitsche at Baden-Baden, all over 6 furlongs, the following year. Tikkoo struck again at the Houghton Sales in 1974 when he bought another son of Habitat, a bay out of Hazy Idea from the Cleaboy Stud, for 30,000 guineas. He was again into a big winner, for this colt, named Hittite Glory, proceeded to win two Group 1 races as a two-year-old, the Flying Childers Stakes and the William Hill Middle Park Stakes.

Hittite Glory might have fetched half as much again if he had been sold a year earlier, because 1974 was the year in which the bottom fell out of the bloodstock market. The collapse was the result of the quadrupling of crude oil prices by the Gulf states following the Middle East war of 1973, which had a grave impact on the economies of the oil-importing countries. Although overproduction is a recurring factor, most setbacks to bloodstock prices arise from events extraneous to the industry. In 1956 the decline was the consequence of international tension caused by the suppression of the Hungarian revolution and the Suez affair. In 1965 bloodstock prices fell in sympathy with the generally depressing economic situation and the imposition of a credit squeeze and Capital Gains Tax. In 1967 the December Sales were affected adversely by an outbreak of foot-and-mouth disease which restricted the movement of horses in some parts of the country. However, the effects of the oil-price crisis of 1974 were much more swingeing than any of these. The loss of confidence in the British economy as a whole was reflected in a headlong fall in the London Stock Exchange FT index from a high of 550 to 150. Bloodstock prices escaped more lightly. Nevertheless Tattersalls' turnover fell by £5.5m. to 9,831,937 guineas, and the average price for all lots sold in the Park Paddocks from 4488 to 2945 guineas. The worst affected were the October Yearling Sales, with a 41% fall in average price compared with 1973. The median price for all yearlings sold at the principal sales in England and Ireland was halved at 1329 guineas, the lowest figure since 1966. This was a particularly alarming reduction because the rise in the median had been failing to keep pace with the rise in average prices for some years, which meant that the gap between the top and bottom of the market was widening and the smaller breeders were operating on increasingly slender margins.

Mares and foals before entering the ring at the December Sales

The only redeeming feature of the Tattersalls scene was the December Sales, whose format had been radically changed. The number of horses sold at these sales had been increasing steadily, and in 1973 the December Sales had overflowed the confines of a single week for the first time with a special sale of American fillies held on the preceding Saturday. The 1974 reorganization involved three days' selling of foals and yearlings at the end of one week, Thursday to Saturday 28–30 November, and five days' selling of broodmares, fillies and horses in training the next week, Monday to Friday 2–6 December. Thanks largely to strong overseas interest, the fall in average prices at these revamped sales was limited to 27%. There was even the excitement of a new record price for a filly-in-training when the Northern Dancer filly Northern Gem was bought by Heron Bloodstock Services for 108,000 guineas – 2000 guineas more than the previous record realized by the Oaks winner Ginevra two years earlier. Buyers and vendors heartily approved the changes. Formerly horses of all categories had been jumbled up in the catalogue, and the new segregation enabled all parties to concentrate on the categories in which they were interested.

The better omens discernible in the 1974 December Sales were not misleading. Although Tattersalls' first three sales of 1975 showed a further decline, prices began to pick up, albeit unevenly, in the autumn. There was encouragement to be drawn from the recovery of the FT index to 400 during the year. However, British investors, still in a state of shock and with their financial wings clipped by the imposition of VAT, mostly remained on the sidelines. The slight recovery was due almost entirely to overseas buyers seeking yearlings and broodmares of quality, and the improvement of prices was concentrated at the top of the market.

It was not until 1977 that Tattersalls' turnover exceeded the 1973 level, reaching 18,759,969 guineas, or £3m. above the previous best. The advance of prices at the Houghton Sales was sensational, with the aggregate at 6,996,940 guineas (up 70%) and the average at 14,164 guineas (up 43%), the disparity between the percentage increases being due to the fact that 78 more lots were sold than the previous year. A new European record yearling price was achieved by the Lyphard colt Lychnis (afterwards renamed Link), from Comte Roland de Chambure's Haras d'Etreham, who was knocked down to Robert Sangster for 250,000 guineas. Earlier that year Sangster had won his first Derby with The Minstrel and his first Prix de l'Arc de Triomphe with Alleged, and was cutting an ever more prominent figure on the international bloodstock scene.

Most observers were probably not aware of it at the time, but they were witnessing the initial stages of the steepest and most sustained escalation of bloodstock prices in the history of the thoroughbred. The oil price rise of 1974 had been responsible for recession in the leading industrial countries, and had the additional dire consequence of initiating world-wide rampant inflation. Bloodstock, like other commodities, shared in this inflation. But the rise in bloodstock prices consistently outstripped general inflation because a number of shrewd investors saw high-class throroughbreds as a hedge against that general inflation. Robert Sangster was one of the first to recognize this potential, propounding and practising vigorously the doctrine that thoroughbreds were an excellent medium of investment, not only because they were in constant demand but because of the ease with which they could be moved from one part of the world to another to take advantage of regional market fluctuations. Although the main weight of Sangster's buying was directed towards the principal North American yearling sales, he remained active in the home market.

If Sangster took the lead, his example was eagerly followed by numbers of Arabs who had accumulated riches beyond the most avaricious dreams of ordinary mortals – mainly, but not exclusively, from oil revenues. The impact of the Arabs on the yearling market began to be felt in the late 1970s, with the Saudi Prince Khalid Abdulla and the Maktoum brothers from Dubai the trend-setters. At the Houghton Sales in 1978 Khalid Abdulla, through his agent the retired trainer Humphrey Cottrill, set a new European yearling record when he bought one of the first crop of the Derby winner Grundy, a chestnut colt out of Parsimony, for 264,000 guineas, a price which prompted Ken Watt to comment musingly from the rostrum: 'Quite a figure, isn't it?' The colt was named Sand Hawk. At the same sales a year later the Haras d'Etreham won back the record when the Lyphard colt Sylver (afterwards renamed Ghadeer) was purchased by the Newmarket trainer Tom Jones, on behalf of Hamdan Al Maktoum, for 625,000 guineas. The hazards of paying huge prices for yearlings and the unpredictability of the progress of young thoroughbreds were vividly illustrated by the fact that Link, Sand Hawk and Ghadeer won only one small race each in England, though Ghadeer added a victory in a small French race as a four-year-old. On the other hand, the high prices do also catch many of the potential star performers, as the Arabs themselves are well aware. For example, Wassl, bought for 300,000 guineas by the Curragh Bloodstock Agency for Ahmed Al Maktoum at the Highflyer Sales in 1951, won the Airlie/Coolmore Irish 2000 Guineas two years later to prove himself one of the best milers in Europe. Some relatively cheap yearlings bought by or for Arabs at the same sales turned out exceptionally well. There was Habibti, purchased by Mohammed Mutawa for 140,000 guineas, who became a champion sprinter: and High Hawk, purchased by the Curragh Bloodstock Agency for 31,000 guineas for Sheikh Mohammed, who became a top-class staying three-year-old filly and won the Group 1 Premio Roma. And at those same sales a year later James Delahooke bought Lear Fan for 64,000 guineas on behalf of Ahmed Salman; Lear Fan proceeded to win the Group 2 Laurent Perrier Champagne Stakes at Doncaster as a two-year-old and the Group 1 Prix Jacques le Marois at Deauville the next year. The principal Arab owners, with their entourages of agents, trainers, stud and racing managers and miscellaneous advisers, became regular features of the Park Paddocks scene during the yearling as well as the December Sales.

It was this set of factors, comprising a universal fall in the value of money combined with a new and calculated concept of bloodstock investment and the constant upward pressure of seemingly unlimited wealth targeted on top-class thoroughbreds of every category that caused the inflation of bloodstock prices to soar above general inflation. The figures tell the story. In the 10-year period 1975 to 1984 Tattersalls' turnover rose from 10,332,218 to 82,597,657 guineas, or by 700%, and the average price of lots sold at Tattersalls sales rose from 3540 to 26,541 guineas, or by 650%. During the same period the cost of living index rose by 259%, or less than half as much. The experience of the period undoubtedly justified the Sangster concept of the virtue of investment in high-class thoroughbreds.

At a time when bloodstock auction houses in many countries were introducing 'select' sales at which the estimated highest-priced yearlings should be concentrated and Tattersalls were being pressed to follow their example, Ken Watt retorted that Tattersalls had had sales that were select in practice if not in name for many years – and that his firm had indeed originated the idea. He was referring to the long-term policy of building up the Houghton Sales rather than the October Sales as the market for quality yearlings, and transferring the principal vendors from the earlier to the later sales as places became available. After all, the Houghton Sales were the direct lineal descendant of the Doncaster St Leger Sales which had been the most important yearling sales for more than half a century.

However, there was no attempt to insist that this arrangement must stand for all time, like a monument set in concrete. Ken Watt expressed the firm's attitude to change in an interview with Janelle Harding published in the *Thoroughbred Record* in 1984: 'Some people think us a bit slow, because we like to think over a new idea before spending a lot of money doing it, and then do it well. We're always trying to improve. We never say we don't like something just because it's new.'

And Richard Mildmay-White, the youngest of the Tattersalls directors, added: 'Captain Watt has never been averse to what he would term "evolution", rather than radical change – hurry slowly. It's not good, galloping into things.'

As the 1970s progressed Tattersalls received a growing volume of gratuitous advice that the dates of the October and the Houghton Sales should be transposed, the argument being that buyers tended to hold back at the earlier sales in anticipation of being able to buy yearlings of better quality later in the month. Accordingly Tattersalls held a referendum among their vendors in 1976, but decided to make no immediate change when a clear consensus in favour of the switch failed to emerge.

The policy of gradualness was justified. In 1977 the change would have had to be made in the face of considerable opposition. But the views of buyers and vendors alike were subtly but steadily changing, and a fresh referendum in 1980 delivered the unequivocal message that the switch should be made. Thus in 1981, after a postponement of only four years, the former Houghton Sales were brought forward to the dates of the October Sales, from 29 September until 2 October, and renamed the Premier Sales; and the former October Sales were put back to the Houghton week, from 13 to 17 October, and renamed the October Open Sales.

The change was an immediate success. The Premier Sales were in the week before the great French international race, the Prix de l'Arc de Triomphe, which is invariably a magnet for prominent members of the racing communities all over the world. These free spenders found the near-concurrence of these two important events extremely convenient. Turnover at the Premier Sales was up 29.2% compared with the Houghton Sales the previous year, in spite of the fact that 83 fewer yearlings were sold, and the average price increased by no less than 57.5%. The run on the progeny of the leading British-based stallion Mill Reef, who realized five of the top fifteen prices, made a powerful contribution to the upward trend. The bay colt Mill Reef out of Arkadina, a mare who had been placed in three Classic races, inspired a duel between the representatives of Robert Sangster and Sheikh Mohammed before the former had the last nod at the new yearling record price of 640,000 guineas; and the representative of Sheikh Mohammed again left the field to a rival when the colt by Mill Reef out of the July Cup winner Parsimony was knocked down to the representative of another Arab, Kais Al-Said, for 460,000 guineas. Moreover the most sanguine expectations of the new October Open Sales were fulfilled, with turnover up

35.9% and the average price up 43.3% on the old October Sales of 1980.

In subsequent years refinements were made to the basic formula of Tattersalls' yearling sales. In 1982 the word 'Highflyer' was added to the title of the Premier Sales to commemorate the great racehorse and stallion who did so much to make the fortune of the founder of the firm. Two years later 'Premier' was dropped so that the title became simply the Highflyer Sales. In 1983 a more fundamental change had been made with the division of the Highflyer Sales into two parts, Part I being intended as a true elite of the season's yearlings selected on both pedigree and conformation. The former system, by which the selection process had been operated by the vendors themselves, had been superseded by a new system in which all the yearlings offered for sale were first graded on pedigree by a Tattersalls committee and then inspected by teams of Tattersalls auctioneers who covered every stud concerned in Britain and Ireland. The inspections were carried out in May and June, and in doubtful cases the teams would return for a second examination in order to determine which sale would be appropriate. There was a record number of 1750 yearlings to be inspected in 1986, and among so many inevitably there were some suffering from illness or injury or merely physically retarded, who could not be properly assessed on the first visit. However, Richard Mildmay-White, who shouldered the main responsibility for categorizing the pedigrees during a 3-week period up to mid-April, had no doubt that first impressions usually prove correct.

The first Part I Sales were as instantly successful as the first Highflyer Sales had been. During seven hours of hectic trading on the afternoon of Tuesday 27 September, 107 yearlings were sold for a total of 16,219,000 guineas and a previously unimaginable average of 151,579 guineas. The aggregate was more than the total for the entire four days of the Highflyer Sales a year earlier. By the end of the week the total had reached 25,541,000 guineas, 9.5m. guineas more than in 1982 in spite of the fact that the concentration on quality meant that 90 fewer yearlings were on offer. The yearlings sold included the first three ever to realize a million guineas in Europe, with the top price of 1,550,000 guineas paid for the colt by Hello Gorgeous out of Centre Piece, afterwards named Hero

Commanche Run with Lester Piggott after winning the Benson and Hedges Gold Cup at York in 1985. He realized 9000 guineas as a yearling at the Newmarket October Sales in 1982

Worship, by a syndicate headed by Robert Sangster.

In 1984 the time-honoured system of selling the lots from individual studs consecutively was abolished. The system of selling block consignments had meant that new vendors, though perhaps offering yearlings of the highest class, might have to wait years to work their way through to the most favoured places in the catalogue as a result of the gradual withdrawal of older or longer-established competitors. This was seen to be clearly inequitable in an age when many new suppliers of quality yearlings were coming to the market. For this reason a new and fairer system was introduced of splitting up the lots from individual studs and dispersing them through the whole catalogue in accordance with a complicated formula of rotation and alphabetical order. In future no consignor could monopolize the best places, nor could new breeders of quality horses be denied their fair share of the limelight.

Meanwhile the October Sales, in their old and new forms, were continuing to yield some marvellous bargains. In 1978 Moorestyle was bought for 4000 guineas and proceeded to win four Group 1 races, including the Prix de la Forêt over 7 furlongs at Longchamp twice. The following year Kalaglow was bought for 11,500 guineas and developed into a top-ranking four-year-old, with victories in two Group 1 races, the Coral Eclipse Stakes and the King George VI and Queen Elizabeth Stakes, to his credit. Two years later again Never So Bold, having changed hands for 9000 guineas as a foal at the December Sales, was bought for 28,000 guineas and became a champion sprinter; and in 1982 Commanche Run was bought for 9000 guineas and went on to win the St Leger, developing into an outstanding middle-distance performer as a four-year-old.

Never So Bold provided an apt example, with a happy ending, of a growing trend in the bloodstock market, which involves the purchase of foals and their resale as yearlings. A number of specialist operators were attracted to this trade, some of them displaying remarkable skill and perspicacity in the selection of those foals with the potential for profitable resale a year later; conversely those who, lacking the necessary skill and experience, attempted to dabble in this kind of market activity were liable to end up with burnt fingers.

Nor was Never So Bold by any means the only subject of this trade which brought satisfaction to both the first and the second buyer. Another example was the colt by Habitat out of Splashing who was submitted by Mr and Mrs Dare Wigan as a foal at the December Sales in 1982. He was bought by Walter Brophy, assistant manager to the leading Irish breeder Tim Rogers, for 85,000 guineas. He was submitted again by Rogers's Loughbrown Stud at the Highflyer Premier Sales the following year, and was bought by the BBA for 320,000 guineas. He was named Bassenthwaite and a year later again returned to Newmarket to win the Group 1 Middle Park Stakes and prove himself one of the fastest of his age group.

The increase in the importance of foal sales was a feature of Tattersalls' trading patterns in the second half of the twentieth century. It was not until 1957 that the number of foals sold annually exceeded the highest pre-war figure, passing the 200 mark for the first time to reach a total of 235. The numbers continued to increase during the next decade, and in 1968 the importance of the foal sales was emphasized by the fact that the 440 horses of that age sold at the December Sales included a filly by Exbury out of Loose Cover who realized 37,000 guineas, a world record price for a foal and the highest price of the week for a horse of any age. The filly was bought by the BBA for export to the USA, where she won five races under the name of Canterbury Tale. Six years later a colt foal by Tudor Melody out of Pelting realized 32,000 guineas, a record for a colt foal sold in Great Britain. This colt was consigned by Mr and Mrs Dare Wigan, who were to make another deep impact on the foal market with the sale of the future Bassenthwaite. The division of the December Sales the next year, with the foals and yearlings at the end of one week and the remaining categories the next week, was to a considerable extent a reflection of the enhanced importance and volume of the foal sales.

Foal prices soared in step with the general escalation of the bloodstock market in the 1970s and 1980s. The price realized by the future Bassenthwaite, though certainly substantial, was not the highest for a foal in 1982, as a colt by the Derby winner Roberto out of the 1000 Guineas winner Enstone Spark fetched nearly twice as much at 165,000 guineas. The average foal price was in five figures for the first time. The escalation continued. In 1984 569 foals were sold at the December Sales for an average of 16,275 guineas, and the foal aggregate of 9,260,560 guineas was more than the aggregate for the whole December Sales as recently as 1977. The chestnut filly by the Derby winner Golden Fleece out of Chemise and so a half-sister of the American champion Erin's Isle inspired a sustained bidding duel between the agents Tim Vigors and Billy Mcdonald, and the price rose to 490,000 guineas before she was knocked down to Vigors. This was a European record price for a foal. Such was the strength of the market that four other foals realized more than 300,000 guineas. The top-priced foal at the 1985 December Sales fell only a little short of the 1984 record when the colt by the Irish Sweeps Derby winner Shareef Dancer out of Chappelle Blanche, submitted by the bloodstock investment firm Bloodstock Breeders PLC, was bought by the Derrinstown Stud for 470,000 guineas.

The reverse side of the advance of the foal sales was a falling-off of the trade in stallions and horses-in-training at the December Sales. In 1976 the stallion Right Tack, who had brought off the unique double of the 2000 Guineas and the Irish 2000 Guineas seven years earlier, established a record stallion price of 70,000 guineas for the December Sales when he was bought by the Susan Piggott Agency for export to

The champion sprinter Never So Bold (Steve Cauthen) winning the Norcros July Cup in 1985. He was sold twice by Tattersalls, realizing 9000 guineas as a foal at the December Sales in 1980 and 28,000 guineas at the October Sales the following year

Australia. Two years later the eight-year-old stallion Filiberto, a son of Ribot, was sold for only 5000 guineas less for export to Canada; and at the same sales the three-year-old filly Swiss Maid, winner of the Champion Stakes, was sold for 325,000 guineas and the two-year-old Galaxy Libra, winner of a race at Ascot that autumn, was sold for 145,000 guineas, thus breaking the record for a colt-in-training set by Vaguely Noble eleven years earlier. In due course Galaxy Libra justified that high price, because as a five-year-old he won two Grade 1 Stakes in the United States, the Sunset Handicap and the Man o' War Stakes. Nevertheless the practice of consigning high-class stallions to the December Sales was on the wane, and sales of horses-in-training were being transferred to the Autumn Sales held at the end of October or early in November. By 1980 the number of horses-in-training sold at the December sales was down to twenty.

The December Sales market in stallions had a temporary and somewhat bizarre resurgence in 1982 when the seven-year-old Acamas was sold for 125,000 guineas, almost twice the record set by Right Tack. Acamas had been the last Classic winner bred and owned by the great French breeder Marcel Boussac when he won the French Derby. Boussac was bankrupt at the time and Acamas passed into the joint ownership of the Aga Khan and the leading Irish breeder Captain Tim Rogers. In looks, Acamas was an almost perfect model of a high-class thoroughbred, but he was also almost completely infertile and his four stud seasons in Ireland yielded only ten live foals. If he had had anything like normal fertility his value would have been many millions of pounds sterling. The tailpiece to the story is that he was exported to France, where he failed again as a stallion and suffered the indignity of being put back into training at the age of 8 and being beaten in three races, finishing ignominiously down the field in the Prix de l'Arc de Triomphe. He was last heard of at stud in Japan.

The Autumn Sales had developed as mixed sales, but the horses-in-training gradually increased in importance at the expense of the other ingredients. By 1976 the *Bloodstock Breeders Review* was describing the one-day mixed sale, involving mares and foals, as a 'dismal affair', with only 41 lots sold, whereas more than 300 horses-in-training were sold during the subsequent three days. From the following year the Autumn Sales were confined to horses in training and yearlings. Even the yearling element came close to extinction in the early 1980s, with only 28 horses of that age sold in 1982. However, the yearling trade began to pick up strongly from that low point as more and more horses of that age came to the market. By 1985 the yearling element of the Autumn Sales covered two days and was given a separate catalogue; and trade was so brisk that 222 yearlings were sold for 678,130 guineas and an average of 3055 guineas. At the same time the prestige of the Autumn Sales as the principal market for horses-in-training continued to increase. Foreign interest was strong, and National Hunt trainers regarded the Autumn Sales as a useful source of high-class potential hurdling talent. In 1985, 420 horses in training were sold, both the aggregate of 3,482,773 guineas and the average of 8292 guineas being records.

In 1966 Tattersalls introduced sales of stallion shares and nominations as a new kind of service to the breeding industry. Three sessions were held during October Sales week and another during the Autumn Sales. Altogether 19 shares and 44 nominations were sold, with the best prices £7100 for a share in St Paddy, £6500 for a share in Crepello and £4300 for a share in Mourne.

From 1967 the sales of shares and nominations were held in London, first at the Hyde Park Hotel and later at the Berkeley Hotel. They were held normally in November and January, with a telephone link to Dublin arranged in conjunction with Goffs for the convenience of Irish breeders. At first they were hailed with enthusiasm as a means of letting fresh air into the stuffy and restrictive atmosphere in which shares and nominations had been exchanged in the past, and as a method of determining true market value. At times shares in and nominations to some of the most popular stallions were exchanged. In 1971, for example, two shares in Tudor Melody, who had sired the 2000 Guineas winner Kashmir II and was one of the most successful speedy stallions, were sold for £16,500 and £14,500; and two nominations to the same stallion were sold for £5000 each. However, doubts began to creep in as time went by. It appeared to be questionable whether the sale of shares and nominations at a particular place and time really did give a fair indication of overall value; they might indeed be inimical to the interests of the majority of share-owners. Moreover the growing practice of selling nominations with 'no foal no fee' and other concessions complicated the calculation of real nomination prices. A decline set in, although shares and nominations to certain stallions, like the 2000 Guineas winner and eminent Classic stallion High Top, continued to appear regularly in the sales catalogues and to be the subject of active trading. At the Berkeley Hotel in January 1983 a share in High Top accounted for £30,000 of the £40,300 realized by six shares, while two nominations to him for £12,000 each were the largest contribution by any stallion to the total of £133,310 realized by 48 nominations.

A year later, with High Top unrepresented, five shares were sold for £23,000 and 47 nominations for £69,800. In view of the sky-high prices being paid for stallion shares and nominations generally, this kind of trade was so insignificant as to be scarcely worthwhile, and Tattersalls decided to discontinue this sector of their business.

In 1979 Tattersalls moved into Ireland through a link with the Ballsbridge International Bloodstock Sales Ltd. The Ballsbridge Sales company had been formed a year earlier when Goffs, who had had a monopoly of bloodstock sales in

Ireland for many years, moved to a newly constructed sales complex at Kill near Naas. The Ballsbridge Sales operation was established by Michael Opperman just across the road from the former Goffs site in the southern suburbs of Dublin.

The link was proposed to Tattersalls by Opperman because there was a danger of the Irish Government imposing a tax on yearlings going to England and, as Irish yearlings formed an important part of Tattersalls' trade, it seemed prudent to obtain a foothold in Ireland. Initially Tattersalls took a 44% interest in the Ballsbridge company, which became Ballsbridge Tattersalls as a result of the merger. Later the same year Opperman resigned as managing director and was succeeded by the veterinary surgeon Willie O'Rourke. In 1985 there was a further change as Tattersalls increased their holding and the operation became a wholly owned subsidiary with the name of 'Tattersalls (Ireland)', Denis Mahony, who was also head of the Dublin firm of estate agents Keane Mahony Smith, being chairman and O'Rourke managing director. Tattersalls (Ireland) moved out of the Royal Dublin Society grounds into new offices at 14 Clyde Road, close to the sale ring in Ballsbridge.

The Ballsbridge operation did not pose a serious challenge to Goffs on the flat racing side. In 1985, for example, Tattersalls (Ireland) sold 201 yearlings for 892,508 guineas at their September Sales, while Goffs sold 724 yearlings for 17,939,320 guineas during the year: and to put the Goffs figures in true perspective it is necessary to add that Tattersalls' aggregate for the year in England was 1379 yearlings for 41,631,034 guineas. The Tattersalls (Ireland) share of the Irish flat race yearling market was no more than useful and regular. The spectacular growth of Ballsbridge Tattersalls and Tattersalls (Ireland) was on the National Hunt side, particularly at the 'Derby Sale' held at the end of June. Turnover at this sale rose from 549,880 to 1,897,650 guineas between 1979 and 1985, with the average price realized almost doubling to 8041 guineas during the same period. The comment in *Horse and Hound* that the Derby Sale was 'the premier outlet for jumping stock' was no exaggeration. Recognizing the strength of the market there, British breeders of National Hunt horses began to join Irish breeders as suppliers to the Derby Sale. The fact that the National Hunt 'stores' submitted there were subject not only to initial selection but to rigorous inspection by a team of veterinary surgeons on arrival at the sales helped to inspire potential buyers with the confidence that they could bid for sound horses of good conformation.

A potentially momentous event occurred in the autumn of 1986 when Tattersalls acquired the Old Fairyhouse Stud at Ratoath in County Meath, 15 miles north-west of Dublin and close to Fairyhouse racecourse where the Irish Grand National is run. The Simmonscourt extension of the Royal Dublin Society where Tattersalls (Ireland) had been holding sales had not been wholly satisfactory, and the development of a modern sales complex on the new property offered much better scope for expansion of business in an Irish bloodstock market which had seen healthy growth as a result of the greatly increased number of quality stallions in the country.

In 1986 Tattersalls had a programme of seven sales in the Park Paddocks comprising the July Sales (mixed): the September Sales (horses in training): the Highflyer Sales (yearlings): the October Sales (yearlings): the Autumn Sales (horses-in-training and yearlings): the December Sales Part I (yearlings and foals): and the December Sales Part II (mares, etc.).

4
The Lot 116 Case

ANY definition must be judged on its brevity, its clarity and its certainty. By this criterion what definition could be less ambiguous or more admirable than that of an auction given in item (1) of the Conditions of Sales promulgated by Messrs Tattersall in the first half of the nineteenth century? It ran:

> The highest bidder to be the purchaser; and if any dispute arise between any two or more bidders, the lot so disputed shall be immediately put up again, and resold.

Tattersalls' Conditions of Sale in force in 1985 did not include the opening and most elementary part of the original definition, but embroidered on the auctioneer's function in cases of dispute. Condition of Sale 1(c) stated:

> The auctioneer is the sole arbiter as to the existence or otherwise of any dispute and if any dispute arise between two or more bidders the Lot so disputed shall be immediately put up again and resold.

There is no equivocation in that condition, as far as it goes. It is the prerogative of the auctioneer to decide whether a dispute exists, and when there is a dispute between bidders there must be an immediate resale. At Tattersalls, resales after two persons have claimed to have made the final bid are ordered six or seven times a year. But what should happen when the dispute is not between two or more bidders, but between one bidder and the auctioneer? The problem then becomes infinitely more complicated and difficult to resolve. Should the auctioneer attempt to settle the dispute by direct consultation with the bidder, order an immediate resale, or seek some other solution that may seem appropriate in the circumstances? The Conditions of Sale do not give a single, unequivocal answer.

It is infinitely to the credit of the competence of the auctioneers and the probity of both parties that disputes between auctioneers and bidders have been exceedingly rare in the history of Tattersalls. Those that have occurred have mostly had farcical overtones. 'Vigilant's Note-Book' in *The Sportsman* recorded one of these farces in its obituary of Edmund Tattersall in March 1898. The scene was the Doncaster St Leger Sales and involved one of the comical characters who seemingly frequented the sales in those days:

The man appeared at the ringside after an early and apparently rather strong luncheon, and out of mere 'bounce' made an offer of a small amount for a weedy little colt that had been brought into the enclosure. To his dismay no increase on his bid was made, and his despairing look as the 'no advance on fifty?' stage was reached brought all lookers-on to a broad grin. They fairly roared when, no longer able to bear the mental agony he was enduring, the man took to his heels and disappeared over the wall of the enclosure. No one laughed louder than Mr Edmund.

Presumably the 'weedy little colt' was put up for immediate resale. The Lot 116 case, the most notorious example of a dispute between auctioneer and bidder, was no laughing matter; and from an apparently straightforward issue between auctioneer and bidder it exploded into a dispute between auctioneer and vendor and a court case with far-reaching implications for all auction houses, whether their main business was concerned with bloodstock, other kinds of livestock, fine arts, or whatever. The occasion was Part I of the Highflyer Premier Sales on the afternoon of 27 September 1983. Lot 116 was a bay or brown colt by Riverman (USA) out of Celerity (FR), the vendor was Alchemy (International) Ltd of New Bond Street, London, the apparently successful bidder was James Flood, and the auctioneer was Ken Watt himself.

In order to understand the convoluted details of the case it is necessary to know something of the background and the events that preceded the sale. Alchemy (International) Ltd was a company registered in Liechtenstein and was a member of a large group of companies based principally in the United States which raised bloodstock world-wide and had farms in Kentucky, Normandy and South Africa. The Alchemy farm in Kentucky was situated on the Old Frankfort Pike at

Versailles, and normally housed a number of stallions, which for the 1986 covering season, for example, included the French Derby winner Caracolero, Mount Hagen and Lydian, who had been racehorses of merit but were somewhat below the top echelon as stallions. In 1982 Alchemy (International) Ltd, whose directors were Maurice Lydchi and Melvyn Walters, entered into an agreement with the Newmarket trainer Henry Cecil to buy foals for resale as yearlings. Anthony Cherry-Downes, known as 'Tote', was also to participate in the operation. The foals were to be sent, for preparation for sale as yearlings, to the Cliff Stud in Yorkshire, which was managed by Henry Cecil's identical twin brother David. The stud was owned by Henry's father-in-law, the famous trainer Sir Noel Murless, and leased by a company of which Henry, his wife Julie and Tote Cherry-Downes were directors.

The omens for the operation looked favourable. Henry Cecil, who had been leading British trainer of winners twice already and headed the list again in 1982, was blessed with a remarkable understanding of thoroughbreds. Tote Cherry-Downes had a particularly keen eye for young horses and was no slave to the fashionable pedigrees which sent prices soaring in the sale ring; he had an enviable record of buying for reasonable prices yearlings which turned out better racehorses than their pedigrees predicted. Cliff Stud was situated at Helmsley in the midst of that part of Yorkshire which had nurtured the original evolution of the thoroughbred from mixed Eastern and native bloodlines.

The Riverman–Celerity colt was one of six foals bought for this new venture in 1982 – four in the United States and two in Britain. He was knocked down to Cherry-Downes for $95,000 (about £62,000 at the current rate of exchange) at the Fasig-Tipton Fall Mixed Sale in November. The price certainly did not seem excessive because Riverman, who had himself won the French 2000 Guineas and had begun his stud career in France with conspicuous success before being transferred to Kentucky in 1977, had proved himself a top-class stallion and had two winners of the Prix de l'Arc de Triomphe, Detroit and Gold River, the French Derby winner Policeman and the French 2000 Guineas winner Irish River to his credit. The price, indeed, was little more than half the average realized by Riverman foals in the United States that year. Nor was he the most expensive of the foals purchased by Alchemy; that dubious honour belonged to a filly by Irish River out of Sarah Percy, acquired by Alchemy for $160,000 at the Keeneland November Breeding Stock Sale.

By the time that the Riverman colt came into the ring at the Park Paddocks at about 7.55 p.m. on 27 September 1983 the resale operation was in some disarray. The Irish River filly, who had been sold 2½ hours earlier, had realized only 50,000 guineas, which meant a paper loss of about £55,000, apart from the cost of transport from Kentucky and her keep for a year. Consequently the Riverman colt had a heavy responsibility to redress the balance. Both Richard Mildmay-White, who had seen him on his selection tour, and Ken Watt, who had examined him after his arrival at the Park Paddocks as he was to sell him, were of the opinion that he was an attractive, high-class colt, but not a potential sales-topper because he had a rather plain head and a slightly dipped back. Two colts, one by Troy and the other by General Assembly, had passed the million-guineas mark earlier in the sale, and it was significant that the reserve price fixed for the Riverman colt was not more than 150,000 guineas. The probable sales-topper, an exceptionally handsome and well-bred colt by Hello Gorgeous out of Centre Piece, was Lot 117 and therefore due to come into the ring immediately after the Riverman colt.

It was no doubt on account of the imminence of the sale of the Hello Gorgeous colt that the bidding for Lot 116 was recorded on audio tape and much, but unfortunately not quite all, of the action was recorded on video film. The tape begins with a typically succinct introduction to the Riverman colt by Ken Watt:

Yearling from the Cliff Stud and a partnership property. Now here is a lovely colt. A bay or brown by Riverman out of Celerity by Dancer's Image, the second dam Calahorra. Dam won two races. Calahorra won six races in France and also placed at Ascot. Very good to follow this colt. He'll make a lovely three-year-old. By Riverman, you know all about him. I'm bid 100,000 for him. 100,000 now for this Riverman colt. We have very few of them to offer you.

James Flood, who was to make the final bid, entered the bidding at 150,000 guineas, the reserve price. Ken Watt did not know him, and at first missed his attempt to bid, so that his attention had to be directed to him by one of the spotters. Then he acknowledged the bid:

Thank you sir. Yes. Under the window. 150,000, I have taken it under the window.

As the early bidders dropped out, the main battle of the bidding was joined at about the 300,000-guineas mark between Flood and Omar Assi, the representative of Maktoum-Al-Maktoum, the eldest of the Maktoum brothers from Dubai. At 380,000 the bid was Flood's. The audio tape recorded Ken Watt's voice in the concluding stages:

380 now. Perhaps 400? 400,000, thank you. That's 4 now for him. 410, 410. At 410. One more? 420. 430. 430. Quite done now. At 430. Perhaps one more? No. 430. I sell right behind at 430. Any more right? Bid's in the window. At 430,000 guineas.

And then the hammer dropped.

As neither Ken Watt nor any of his colleagues on the rostrum knew Flood he was unable to name the successful bidder. While Lot 116 was led out and Watt prepared to sell 117, Michael Hillman, from the staff of Ballsbridge Tattersalls Ltd and acting as 'runner' on this occasion, was despatched to obtain the buyer's signature on the confirmatory sales form, together with his name and address. Hillman met Flood at the foot of the stairs leading from the bidder's enclosure, but when he presented the form Flood denied making the final bid, though admitting that he had bid 410,000 guineas. Accordingly Hillman invited him to come round to the back of the rostrum to discuss the matter with the auctioneer.

By the time Hillman, Flood and Flood's friend Hugh Boyle had reached the back of the rostrum Ken Watt had sold the Hello Gorgeous colt for the new European record yearling price of 1,550,000 guineas, thereby concluding his stint of selling, and had handed over to the next auctioneer, Sir Peter Nugent. Accordingly he was available to leave the rostrum and speak to Flood. An interview lasting about five minutes ensued, during which Watt repeatedly asserted that Flood had bid 430,000 and Flood as repeatedly denied it. Watt then decided that he must obtain confirmation of his opinion from the spotters and broke off the discussion, requesting Flood to return in 10 minutes' time. This Flood promised to do, but in fact he disappeared and was not seen in the Park Paddocks again.

Ken Watt found his spotter David Batten and those of his own colleagues who had been on the rostrum unanimous that the final bid of 430,000 guineas had come from the man whose name they subsequently discovered to be James Flood. Watt was in a dilemma. If the dispute had been between two individuals who both claimed to have made the final bid he would have resold the colt without delay; but this situation was altogether different. The clear final bidder had repudiated his bid, time had elapsed and more lots had been sold, and the end of the day's session was rapidly approaching; there were only nine more yearlings to be sold after Lot 117 and it would all be over by 8.45 p.m. Ken Watt sent for his consultant and legal adviser Geoffrey Hart and they held a hurried conference at the back of the rostrum. Watt had to be sure what options were open to him in the unprecedented circumstances. Everything hinged on the 4th Condition of Sale, which read:

4th – The Purchaser of each Lot shall –

(a) give his name and address to TATTERSALLS if so required.
(b) take away at his own expense every Lot purchased by him, the day following the Sale of that Lot.
(c) pay the full amount of the purchase price to TATTERSALLS before removing any Lot purchased by him, and if the purchaser shall fail to comply with any of Conditions 4 (a), (b) and (c) above the Lot may be re-sold immediately or otherwise by public or private sale and the deficiency (if any) attending such resale shall be made good by the defaulting purchaser on demand by TATTERSALLS.

Hart confirmed that the final bidder (Flood) had reneged on his contract, and that this was not affected by his refusal to sign the slip; the contract was the fall of the hammer. Watt was entitled to resell the colt by either public or private sale.

Soon after this consultation Watt abandoned the option of immediate re-auction, because it would not be in the best interests of the vendor. There was an air of anticlimax after the sale of Lot 117; the building was beginning to empty as potential bidders began to drift away for dinner, and the chances of the Riverman colt making anything like the same price, if he were submitted again that evening, were becoming increasingly remote. As a search of the Park Paddocks had failed to discover any trace of Flood and the inference was that he had absconded, Watt's thoughts turned more and more to the expedient of offering the horse to the underbidder as the most promising expedient.

The next problem was to identify the underbidder. Ken Watt knew Omar Assi by sight but did not know his name or which of the main Arab buyers he represented. After some delay his identity was established, and the fact ascertained that he worked for Maktoum-Al-Maktoum and that Maktoum's entourage were staying at the Moat House Hotel in Newmarket. A telephone call was put through to the hotel to Michael Goodbody, an adviser to Maktoum and manager of his Gainsborough Stud near Newbury, to inform him of the circumstances and ask him whether Maktoum would take the colt at the underbid price. Goodbody replied that they would discuss the matter and give their decision in the morning.

The decision was in the negative. Goodbody took the view that the circumstances were suspicious. Some persons, aware of the high prices that the Arabs were prepared to pay, had been known to run up the bidding against them in the past, and this could have been another example of the practice, since the original purchaser could not be found; and Omar Assi's view was that defeat in the bidding for a horse was the end of the matter. A complication arose, because both Omar Assi and Goodbody, who had watched him intently from the opposite side of the sale ring, denied flatly that the former had bid 420,000 guineas, stating that he stopped at 400,000 which was their agreed limit on the horse. Ken Watt and his colleagues did not waver in their belief that Omar Assi had bid 420,000, and this was a direct conflict of opinion that was never explained.

The refusal of Maktoum-Al-Maktoum and his representatives to take the Riverman colt left re-auction as the sole remaining option. Accordingly the colt was put up for sale again on Thursday, two days after the original sale but still one day before the end of the four-day Highflyer Premier Yearling Sales. Tattersalls raised the previous reserve price by 50,000 to 200,000 guineas in the knowledge that there had certainly been more than one genuine bidder above that figure on Tuesday evening. In the event the colt realized precisely the reserve price, at which he was knocked down to Robert Gibbons. Ironically, Gibbons was acting for Maktoum-Al-Maktoum's younger brother Hamdan.

There, it might have been expected, the matter would rest. Although the intervention of a fraudulent and mendacious bidder had raised the price of Lot 116 to an artificially high level on the first occasion, the colt ultimately had realized a sum 50,000 guineas more than the vendors had been ready to accept before the sales began – a satisfactory outcome, it would seem. However, the vendors did not see it in that light. They considered that Tattersalls had been incompetent in their conduct of the selling of the Riverman colt, and had failed in their contractual duty to obtain the best possible price for the colt. They claimed that Tattersalls had been negligent because they had not re-auctioned the colt on the Tuesday evening – before, as far as possible, the same audience of bidders. This, the vendors alleged, would obviously have been the correct and most advantageous course of action.

The allegations of negligence and breach of duty were denied by Tattersalls. The resulting legal case did not reach the High Court in London until 20 months after the notorious sale; so it was on 4 June 1985 that it opened before Mr Justice (The Hon. Sir David) Hirst. The hearing lasted 13 days, and Mr Justice Hirst then deliberated for 4 days before giving judgement on 26 June. The duration of the hearing had been increased by the introduction into the proceeedings of James Flood, against whom Tattersalls would claim an indemnity if they should lose the case.

Although Tatteralls did not know Flood's name at the time of the sale, subsequent investigations, in which the police were involved, had revealed his identity. He had gone to live in the Spanish resort of Marbella for a time after the sale of Lot 116, but was arrested at London Airport on 28 March 1984 and taken to Newmarket police station for questioning concerning allegations of criminal fraud. He was released without being charged, but the episode gave Tattersalls's legal representative the opportunity to serve him with a third-party writ to appear in the case.

The case was covered by the extremely intelligent and painstaking racing journalist Howard Wright, who filled no fewer than fourteen notebooks with his court jottings and wrote a lucid account of the proceedings in the August 1985 issue of *Pacemaker International* magazine. Wright described the opening of the case:

> So the three sides came together at the High Court in London's Strand, gathering their forces in Court 22, a newish, light and airy room which gave the impression of space while retaining the awesome image of British judicial tradition.
>
> At first sight it appeared a simple case, and one could have wondered why Tattersalls were going to the time, trouble and expense of pursuing a defence.

This initial impression of simplicity quickly evaporated as submissions, examinations and cross-examinations of witnesses, and legal arguments wove a web of complexity over the case which became difficult to unravel. An orderly presentation of the unfolding of the court proceedings can be achieved most readily by separating the two main aspects of the case – on the one hand, the attempt to elucidate the behaviour and motives of James Flood at the sale of Lot 116, and on the other hand the attempt by the plaintiffs – Alchemy (International) Ltd – to substantiate allegations of negligence against the defendants, Tattersalls. This approach is the more apt because the plaintiffs found no fault with Tattersalls' conduct of the first sale, and took issue only with their subsequent actions, or lack of action.

The video and tape recordings of the sale of Lot 116 were both played in court. The video was inconclusive. Although it showed some of Flood's bids, the camera panned away from him too soon to reveal whether he made the 430,000 guineas bid, and picked up Omar Assi, who was standing a little sideways with his head bent over his catalogue, as if he had finished bidding. The evidence of the tape was more valuable. As the judge pointed out, Ken Watt had a distinctive voice, and there was an unmistakable difference in tone when it was interrogatory, calling for a bid, and when it was affirmative, acknowledging a bid. The tone when he mentioned '430,000' several times was clearly affirmative, and if he had made a mistake Flood could easily have corrected it by shouting out a denial. In his judgement Mr Justice Hirst found that Flood had bid knowingly and without the intention at the time of honouring his bid; there was no other reasonable explanation of his refusal to give his name and address.

Flood's involvement in the sale, which was the root of all the trouble, was a bizarre deviation from the standards of integrity accepted as normal at Tattersalls' sales – or, for that matter, at any of the sales conducted by the principal European auctioneering houses. On his own admission, he knew little of bloodstock auctions and was a complete stranger to Tattersalls' auctioneers and staff. He was a professional gambler and former bookmaker from Belfast, who claimed to have had books written and films made about him. He also claimed to have a 'flamboyant' personality, though the judge stated that 'bombastic' would be a better word. Yet he appeared in court wearing a sober grey suit, and spoke in a quiet voice with only a trace of an Irish accent. Fair-headed and snub-nosed, he did not cut a formidable figure in the witness box.

In his findings Mr Justice Hirst said of Flood:

> Although his almost boastful admission that he cheats at gambling was engagingly frank, there can be no doubt that Mr Flood has lied on material issues both to the police and to this court. He lied to the police when asserting that he had given his name and address and when feigning ignorance of the hue and cry following the auction. He lied to this court in his repeated assertions in his evidence-in-chief that he thought all figures mentioned by Captain Watt were interrogative, and in some at least of his stories about his means in September 1983. He was also clearly intending to assert that the interview with Captain Watt took place in the few fleeting moments between Lots 116 and 117 to bolster a case that the interview was therefore necessarily brief and perfunctory, until he realised from the evidence of the time that this was untenable and so shifted his stance.

Some of Flood's answers to questions put to him at interviews at Newmarket police station on 28 March 1984, recorded contemporaneously and read out by Detective Chief Inspector Stuart Chapman in court, plumbed the depths of implausibility.

Q. So you are saying you were a genuine bidder?
A. Yes.
Q. What checks had you done on the horse, i.e. veterinary examination, etc.?
A. None. I just heard it was one of three horses worth buying in the sales.

Q. Surely if you had intended to spend that sort of money out, you would have had the horse examined by a vet?
A. No.
Q. Have you got the money to buy such a horse?
A. I haven't got it personally but I could put that sort of money together by getting someone to come in with me.
Q. Nevertheless you had no financial backing?
A. A colt is bought at its cheapest price. It will always fetch more later on, so it's a winner.
Q. I can't believe that.
A. Well, 97 per cent are.

Later in the interview Chief Inspector Chapman recorded the following exchange:

Q. How did you know which horse you were going to buy?
A. I didn't know until the day of the sales, but I knew it was the Highflyer Sales on then.
Q. How did you get a catalogue?
A. I bought one when I arrived at the sales.
Q. So, if you didn't have a catalogue until the day of the sales, how come you knew which horses were there to be bought?
A. It was all in the papers and it was the premier sales.

Later again:

Q. What state were your financial affairs in in September?
A. I couldn't say. They are always up and down.
Q. You must have some idea.
A. I've got no idea within £50,000.
Q. Well, tell us within £50,000.
A. I've got no idea.

When asked why he disappeared after the auction and how he left Newmarket, Flood replied that he got a lift from 'a little fellow who has a wig and drives a Mercedes'; and added: 'He's an old-time boxer. I met him at the sales.' This account of his departure from the sales was presumed to be an excursion into the wilder realms of fantasy. Indeed, the record of the police interviews left the indelible impression that Flood was either astonishingly naïve and ignorant of racing and bloodstock sales or deplorably disingenuous. The court was left in little doubt as to which of those alternatives was correct.

With benefit of hindsight, any close observer of the

bloodstock scene can only wonder that a man described by Ken Watt as a 'mendacious bidder', a petty gambler on the grubby fringe of the racing world, was able to cause such a stir and sow the seeds of litigation between parties who included some of the most honourable men in the business. The plaintiffs' case against Tattersalls on breach of duty and negligence was based on Tatteralls' alleged failure to put the Riverman colt up for auction again immediately after Flood refused to give his name and address or disputed his bid; and alternatively on their failure to put the colt up for auction again immediately after Flood did not return after the ten minute interval. Moreover Tattersalls put the colt up for auction again on the third day of the sales as an additional lot when they knew, or ought to have known, that:

1. The major international purchasers would not be attending the sales on that day.
2. The price likely to be obtained for the colt would be much less than that bid on the first day of the sales, and less than its proper value.

Tattersalls' case in response was that, believing that a valid bid of 430,000 guineas had been made, they could not re-auction the Riverman colt (Lot 116) unless they were satisfied that the bid would not be honoured; once they were so satisfied, the logical course of action was to offer the colt to the underbidder, who had shown strong interest in the colt by entering the bidding at about 300,000 guineas and making alternate bids thereafter; that the underbidder had left the arena after the sale of Lot 117; that there had been a general exodus of potential bidders after the sale of Lot 117 with the result that the market was less buoyant; and that consequently the colt was likely to realize very much less than 430,000 guineas if he were re-auctioned the same evening.

The logic in favour of offering the colt to the underbidder was strong. What Tattersalls could not know during the remainder of Tuesday's selling was that the underbidder would deny having bid 420,000 guineas and decline to take any further interest in the colt. Nor was the logic of the offer to the underbidder accepted by the plaintiffs. In cross-examination Henry Cecil condemned the offer as 'idiotic', and stated that it would have been much better to bring the colt back for resale

The interior of the new sale ring. The area enclosed by the white rails is reserved for intending bidders

as quickly as possible, even if it had been the last lot of the day. He expressed the extravagant opinion that a resale the same evening might have realized 500,000, because it was a good-looking colt.

Neither of the Alchemy directors, Lydchi and Walters, gave evidence, though Walters was in court during most of the proceedings. However, witnesses called by the plaintiffs supported the argument for immediate resale. Two of them, Jonathan Irwin and Colonel Dick Warden, commanded special respect on account of their lively intelligence and intimate understanding of the bloodstock auctioneering business – Irwin as the managing director of the leading Irish bloodstock auction house Goffs, and Warden as a former trainer and current bloodstock agent with an important role as adviser and buyer for Sheikh Mohammed, another of the brothers of Maktoum-Al-Maktoum. Irwin said that at Goffs they would have put the colt up for resale as soon as possible and would not have attempted to contact the underbidder; and Warden stated that it was the usual practice of auctioneers internationally to put the horse back in the sale ring as soon as possible if there was any problem or dispute, and he could not understand why Tattersalls had not done so on this occasion. Both these witnesses, however, made concessions in cross-examination. Asked by Michael Connell, QC, appearing for Tattersalls: 'Is it in your opinion, a perfectly tenable view [first to try and hold the original purchaser to his bid and then get in touch with the underbidder] for them to pursue?' Irwin replied: 'It is understandable, what they did.' And the main part of Warden's cross-examination by Connell concluded with this exchange of questions and answers:

Q. It is a perfectly reasonable thing for the auctioneer to do in that situation [the repudiation of his final bid by Flood] to say to himself, 'The best thing I can do for my client is to keep this man to his bid'.
A. Yes. And, at the same time, to say that there is trouble and the animal will be sold at a certain time to keep the other people on the boil.
Q. You add that, but if you say and publicly announce that the animal will be resold . . .
A. You antagonize the other man.
Q. You have immediately taken the pressure, if I may so put it, off the bidder.
A. That is a risk that is up to the auctioneer.
Q. Does it not come to this, Colonel Warden, at the end of the day, it is a very difficult situation?'
A. Extremely difficult.
Q. And it is very difficult for anybody to say what is the right and the wrong course?
A. Very difficult.
Q. Either of the courses would have been perfectly reasonable?
A. Yes.

The expert witnesses called by Tattersalls included Paul Whitfield, a director of Christies, the fine art dealers. Whitfield stated in conclusion of his written evidence:

Having considered all the material made available to me, I consider that the auctioneer, Captain Watt, an undoubtedly experienced auctioneer, did indeed act prudently both in the conduct of the sale of Lot 116 and in his subsequent actions. I also consider that Tattersalls took the steps that a reasonably prudent company would have done in the circumstances of this case, and in the context of the best standards of auction sales as conducted in this country.

In cross-examination he said that Christies would never re-offer a lot unless the dispute was known before the next lot was put up, since any subsequent re-auction the same day was almost bound to result in a fiasco. However the impact of his evidence was limited by the fact that there were considerable differences between fine art sales and sales of bloodstock; indeed subsequent re-auction the same day was hardly a practicable option at Christies because the same auctioneer remained on the rostrum throughout a sale and therefore would have no opportunity to investigate in circumstances similar to those of Lot 116. The decisive evidence was given by Ken Watt himself and by another of the expert witnesses, Lieutenant-Colonel Robin Hastings, the chairman and managing director of the British Bloodstock Agency. They were both utterly convincing in the witness box, impressing everyone in court by their firmness of tone and air of unimpeachable integrity. Each had an upright and soldierly demeanour. Although Ken Watt had been frustrated by ill health in his ambition for a career in the army, he looked every inch a man with a military background; and Robin Hastings, with the slight build of a man who had ridden successfully in races over fences, had seen distinguished service as a regular officer in the Rifle Brigade in the Second World War, being awarded the DSO and the MC before be began a second career in Britain's biggest bloodstock agency.

In cross-examination by Mr Connell, Ken Watt was asked to comment on the suggestion that he should have made preparatory arrangements for a re-auction immediately after Flood reneged on his bid. He replied that he could not agree that this would have been correct, because there was no dispute in the ordinary sense of the word, but a denial of the bid by the final bidder, which became apparent only after the lot had left the ring. The colt could have come up again at the end of the day but that would not have been a good time or fair to the owner, since in his experience there was a serious stigma attached to a horse that was re-auctioned immediately and it did not make as much money again. He said that overall the best interest of the buyer was not to re-auction immediately, but to try to make the purchaser honour his contract and to seek out the underbidder to see if he was willing to purchase at the underbid price. However, he had definitely considered immediate re-auctioning as one possible course of action.

The core of the evidence given by Robin Hastings was that immediate re-auctioning (that is, before Lot 117), would have been the best course, but this was impossible because the dispute with the purchaser did not arise until after the next lot was in the ring. He stated in his written evidence:

> Of course, with the benefit of hindsight, it might have been possible to have re-submitted the colt there and then, but I must have regard to the facts of the situation, and at the time there were sensible reasons for not doing so: e.g., the lateness of the hour, the fact that the sales room was emptying rapidly, and the fact that the purchaser was not saying that he had not bid at all, only that he had bid 410,000 as opposed to 430,000.

And he added:

> In view of the very limited alternatives open to Tattersalls, bearing in mind the refusal of the underbidder to take the colt, I consider that there was no realistic alternative but to offer the colt again on the third day.

In amplifying his written evidence, Hastings expressed the opinion that an underbidder would usually be disinclined to bid for a re-auctioned lot unless he knew the reason for the re-auction very clearly; and in a case like that of Lot 116 he would be all the more disinclined because he would suspect that there had been some monkey business. One of the most telling pieces of evidence given by Hastings concerned Lots 125 and 126, the last two lots sold that Tuesday evening. They were colts by the Derby winners Troy and Mill Reef and were expected to make high prices. It was only when the bidding became hesitant and they seemed likely to be sold cheaply that the BBA stepped in and bought them for 82,000 and 78,000 guineas respectively. This happened probably because it was late in the evening and many people had gone home. The implications for a putative resale of Lot 116 after the Mill Reef colt were plain, and Hastings said in evidence:

> At that time of the evening certainly the casual buyer had gone and a lot of people would not have heard that he was coming in, and therefore there would be a considerable disadvantage in putting him up then. If the original people who bid for him had wanted him, they would bid for him at any time if they were serious about it.

In the legal arguments that figured prominently in the case much play was made with the precedent of Maynard v. West Midlands Regional Health Authority (1984) which concerned medical negligence in the field of diagnosis and treatment. The Maynard case went to the House of Lords where Lord Scarman, delivering a unanimous judgement, ruled that a case based on an allegation that a fully considered decision of two consultants in the field of their special skill was negligent clearly presented certain difficulties of proof; and it was not enough to show that there is a body of competent professional opinion which considers that there was a wrong decision if there also exists a body of professional opinion, equally competent, which supports the opposite view.

The parallel between 'Maynard' and the Lot 116 case was drawn by Connell. Mr Peter Sheridan, representing Alchemy, claimed that 'Maynard' did not apply, but Mr Justice Hirst rejected his submission. Mr Justice Hirst said that Tattersalls were entitled to be judged on the points of the Maynard case; evidence had come from expert witnesses of high calibre on both sides, and it was his responsibility to decide whether Tattersalls had been in breach of their duty to exercise all reasonable skill and care:

1. To obtain the best price for the vendor's goods.
2. To act in the vendor's best interests.

In giving judgement Mr Justice Hirst allowed due weight to Sheridan's argument that there had been an overwhelming case for immediate re-auction, however late in the day, because of the special nature of the Part I select day in contrast to the other days of the Highflyer Sales, with its abundance both of top-quality horses and top-quality buyers attracted by skilful publicity to attend on that occasion. But he went on:

At the same time, it is perfectly clear that such undoubted special advantages must tend to evaporate, perhaps even to vanishing point, at the end of a very long day, which had started six and a half hours before. Moreover, there was a very special circumstance which was likely to accelerate that process, namely the fact that the biggest lot of the day, 117, with all its attendant excitement, had immediately followed 116 and was completed before Captain Watt first knew of the problem. Indeed, the evidence is abundant that at this stage there had been a large exodus, no doubt in large measure consisting of spectators, but also, I am quite sure, consisting of some buyers, as it was after 8.00 p.m. on an occasion of much social as well as commercial significance.

Quite apart from these considerations, I am very strongly influenced by the stigma aspect, which carried so much weight with Captain Watt and is also so strongly supported by Colonel Hastings. I found Colonel Hastings's reasoning on this point convincing and was unpersuaded by Mr Sheridan's argument that Tattersalls with all their great skill and reputation as auctioneers would necessarily have been capable of allaying this anxiety by a skilful and punctual announcement, though I am sure they would have done their best if the need had arisen.

The very earliest the horse could have been actually re-auctioned was after the conclusion of the Hart consultation – i.e. after Lot 123 and immediately before the last two Lots 125 and 126, 124 having been withdrawn.

But, in fact, I think it would have been quite reasonable for Tattersalls, if they had decided to re-auction, to have balanced the interest of the vendors of those last two lots against that of the vendor of 116 and decided not to offend the former by interposing the Riverman colt before the end. Consequently the likelihood is that if there had been a re-auction it would have been at the very end, after Lot 126 and after 8.40 p.m. and thus at the worst possible time on that particular day.

In my judgement, applying Colonel Hastings's very careful reasoning, the better view on balance is that a re-auction at that juncture was more likely than not to be disadvantageous to the vendor.

This summary of the events of the fateful evening of 27 September 1983 and the options that had been available to Ken Watt after James Flood's denial of his final bid for Lot 116 led Mr Justice Hirst to the conclusion that Alchemy had failed to establish their claim that Tattersalls had acted negligently. Accordingly he entered judgement for Tattersalls against the plaintiffs on the plaintiffs' claim against Tattersalls. There was also judgement for Tattersalls against Flood in the third-party proceedings for an indemnity to cover the shortfall of Tattersalls' expenses, and Flood's contribution claim against Tattersalls was dismissed. At the same time there was judgement for the plaintiffs against Flood for the sterling equivalent of 230,000 guineas (the difference between the sum bid by Flood and the sum realized when the Riverman colt was re-auctioned), that is £241,500, together with interest.

Thus the case had ended with the complete vindication of Tattersalls, and of the conduct of the Lot 116 affair by Ken Watt in particular. The judgement was seen not only as clearing Tattersalls of the allegation of negligence in the special circumstances of Lot 116, but as establishing the precedent that an auctioneer was not necessarily negligent if he decided against immediate re-auction when a dispute arose. For this reason Tattersalls could take the view that they had fought the case successfully on behalf of all auction houses and not merely their own. If the circumstances had been unprecedented, then the outcome of the case was of historic significance.

Mr Justice Hirst had been appointed to preside over the legal proceedings at the eleventh hour. In a very short space of time he had acquired a sure grasp of the intricacies of the case and of the operation of the esoteric world of thoroughbred racing, breeding and auctioneering. Only occasional slips, like a confusion of 'foals' with 'yearlings', betrayed the fact that his command of the appropriate terminology was incomplete. Round of face and twinkling of eye, his treatment of witnesses was patient, sympathetic and good-humoured. He even showed flashes of wit: as when, the day after the Derby, he released Henry Cecil from court with his permission to 'slip anchor'.* At the end of the case he had to make up his mind which set of witnesses, on balance, had carried the day in the play of argument and counter-argument. Although he uttered the words in the specific context of the dispute with Flood, one sentence in his findings summed up his reasons for preferring the arguments put forward on Tattersalls' side on the broad issues of the case:

So far as credibility is concerned, I found all the Tattersalls witnesses who gave evidence entirely honest, straightforward witnesses, who were prepared to make concessions, even if not advantageous to their case, and who approached their evidence in a thoroughly responsible fashion.

There could have been no stronger endorsement of Tattersalls' stand on the question of Lot 116, or of their status as leaders in the field of bloodstock auctioneering not only with respect to the volume of business but also with respect to the

* Cecil had gained his first training success in the Derby with Slip Anchor.

integrity with which that business was conducted. Ken Watt was expressing the views of the firm when he wrote to a friend after the case: 'We need hardly say how we ourselves appreciated the judge's final summing up and verdict; it all made it worth while in justifying two hundred and twenty years of Tattersalls history as an institution of Britain.'

Nick Robinson elucidated one important aspect of the case in his publisher's comment, 'Setting the Pace' in the August 1985 issue of *Pacemaker International* magazine. He wrote:

> Although this case brought some unfavourable publicity to the racing industry . . . . Tattersalls have to be congratulated on pursuing this case to a successful conclusion. Had they lost, the inevitable tightening up on bidding would not have been conducive to optimum prices. The identification of a new bidder is virtually impossible during an auction, and as one sales auction executive said to me last week, 'when we see a new face bidding these days we get excited'. It usually means the Arabs are using an unknown person to throw people off the scent.

Robinson also drew attention to another curious aspect of the case which concerned personalities, some well-known and some not so well-known, 'their names flitting in and out like members of the chorus'. Most of these allusions arose from the activities, real or invented, of James Flood, his 'illusory' syndicate, the people who may have advised him, or for whom he may have been bidding, or who may have been bidding him up. There were plenty of trails, many of them no doubt false, which were laid but never followed through. The scent petered out, or the legal hounds declined to persevere. The greatest unexplained mystery is what Flood was up to. As Mr Justice Hirst remarked: 'His bid was fraudulent and Tattersalls have no need to prove what his motive was. I shall resist the temptation to suggest what it might have been.' Lay observers of the case cannot do better than follow the judge's example.

The racing careers of Lots 116 and 117, the colts whose presence in the Highflyer Premier Yearling Sales of 1983 gave rise to so much controversy, provided one of the more entertaining sequels to the case and exemplified the impossibility of accurate valuation of immature thoroughbreds. Lot 116, the Riverman colt, was regarded by experts at the time of the sale as a well-bred and handsome but less than perfect colt. Lot 117, the Hello Gorgeous colt, was regarded as an individual of supremely high-class looks and conformation. Lot 116, at his second and genuine sale, realized 200,000 guineas; Lot 117 realized the European record yearling price of 1,550,000 guineas. But their racing achievements made a strange and ironic contrast. The Riverman colt, named Sulaafah, won Germany's most important two-year-old race, the Group 2 Moet and Chandon Zukunftsrennen at Baden-Baden, and returned to Baden-Baden the next year to win another important race, the Group 3 Badener Meile. He also won two good races in England. The Hello Gorgeous colt, named Hero Worship, appeared in two races in Ireland as a two-year-old and was unplaced in both of them. By co-incidence, Omar Assi was the underbidder for Lot 117. He was well out of that one.

Finally, it must be recorded that the embarrassment of the Lot 116 case motivated Tattersalls to summon up the latest technological equipment to guard against any repetition of the kind of dispute that had been at the root of the trouble. Video cameras were installed in the sales building which, at the touch of a button beside the auctioneer's desk, would zoom in on the action if suspicion was aroused by an unknown or dubious bidder. A prime example of shutting the stable door after the horse had bolted, it might be said. But it is also fair to say that the circumstances of the Lot 116 case, unprecedented in the forty years of Ken Watt's experience, could not reasonably have been anticipated by installation of the most modern and expensive safeguards against a kind of malpractice whose incidence was infinitely rare.

5

Some Aspects of Auctioneering

THOROUGHBRED auctions are akin to theatrical performances. The auctioneer has to establish the same rapport with the bidder that the actor seeks with his audience, and in order to extract the highest possible price must employ a range of persuasive talents comparable to the range of the actor's craft. He may wheedle, he may hector, he may appeal to the bidder's vanity and at times he may attempt to put ideas of the merit of the lot on offer into the bidder's head. This affinity with the theatre applies to all bloodstock auctions where the prices may climb to the levels of the most select fine art sales, since the thoroughbreds themselves, being animate and highly idiosyncratic creatures, contribute their own vital share to the dramatic action: and is particularly true of bloodstock sales in Britain at which, in contrast to the practice in some foreign countries, all bids are made directly to the auctioneer and the personal relationship between bidder and auctioneer is all-important. The analogy with the theatre is emphasized in the case of Tattersalls by the resemblance of the interior of Richardson's magnificent sales pavilion in the Park Paddocks to a theatre with an auditorium seating 500 and capable of accommodating twice that number altogether.

Tony Morris, writing in the *Racing Post* (30 July 1986), recognized the theatricality of public auctions, but saw it in orchestral rather than histrionic terms:

> You don't have to be totally deranged to see the auctioneer as a conductor, the bidders as a group of avant-garde musicians improvising on a theme, and the fall of the hammer as the end of each movement.

Kenneth Watt in a characteristic pose as he seeks to wheedle another bid

However, to stay with the stage analogy, it is beyond dispute that every great actor has his individual style – the arts of an Olivier and a Gielgud could never be confused – and likewise every successful bloodstock auctioneer has his individual rostrum personality and his individual approach to the problems of cajoling the bidders. The four men who have headed the firm of Tattersalls in the twentieth century – Somerville Tattersall, Gerald Deane, Ken Watt and Michael Watt – have all possessed powers of persuasion that have seemed almost hypnotic at times, but each of them has had a radically different manner on the rostrum. Moreover the whole concept of auctioneering has undergone change in the course of the century. Like journalistic style, auctioneering style has tended to become tauter, more succinct, less long-winded and less discursive. Time has become more precious and the business more urgent. The change can be illustrated most graphically by comparing Ken Watt's brief preliminary statement at the dispersal sale of James A. Dewar's bloodstock at the December Sales in 1954, when he confined himself to three sentences eulogizing Dewar's services to British breeding and expressing the hope that some of the mares would be retained in Britain, with the rambling prolixity of Sommy Tattersall's speech from the rostrum before the sale of Sceptre, the winner of four Classic races, as a twelve-year-old at the July Sales 43 years earlier. After reminding the large crowd round the sale ring that her yearling price of 10,000 guineas still stood as a record, Sommy continued:

At the time I thought she was rather dear, because of her twisted foreleg. I was wrong and Mr Sievier [her purchaser, who retained her until she was four] was right. At the end of her three-year-old career, in King Edward's Coronation year, she came up for sale again, with a reserve of 20,000 on her. I then made some remarks on her value, and advised any rich man present to buy her. I said she would be extremely unlucky if she did not win one of the ten thousand pound races, for she was engaged in three, and came of a stout family, her granddam, Lily Agnes, being an extremely hardy mare, who took part in 32 races, and won 21 of them, and then bred Ormonde, Farewell, and other winners. Sceptre, I went on to say, seemed to have inherited Lily Agnes's disposition. However, she passed out of the ring unsold. Somebody told me afterwards that he did not know how I had the face to make such observations. Well, Sceptre, despite the fact that she had none the best of luck in the Eclipse, as Madden and Martin, who rode in that race, will tell you, won in stakes that year 13,600 guineas. Her produce have each won something, her three-year-old Coronation having been placed.

At the Second Spring Meeting here we sold some of her produce for 10,450 guineas, and I calculate that at present Sir William Bass has obtained a profit of about £4500 before Sceptre and her eldest daughter are sold. Some people look at the matter from a commercial point of view. I do not know what she may be worth from that standpoint, but any rich man who can afford to do so should give 5000 or 6000 guineas extra for the pleasure of seeing Sceptre each day, just as some people spend thousands on pictures. A mare like Sceptre only comes once in 25 years or so. She and her eldest daughter ought not to be allowed to leave the country. We ought to keep this mare and Maid of the Mist in this country. I shall look on English racing people as unpatriotic, like some of our politicians, if they let her go. La Flèche was the record price mare before Sceptre, and she paid her way well. I think she has also paid Sir Tatton Sykes. Her blood has come out in a remarkable way in Swynford. La Flèche very nearly went to France, for there was a certain amount of luck about her going to Sledmere. Had she gone abroad we should have had no Swynford, who throws back to La Flèche in colour.

It is a great mistake for us to allow all the best mares to leave the country. We have permitted a good many of our best stallions to go. The French people recently tried to buy William The Third, but I am very pleased to hear that the Duke of Portland and the Duchess said he was to live and die at Welbeck. The Duke of Portland and Lord Derby were just too late to save Cyllene from exportation to the Argentine.

One of the most exciting races we have seen in recent years was that for the Eclipse Stakes, when Rock Sand and Ard Patrick opposed Sceptre. We have lost the two horses. Let us keep the mare, whom Martin considers the best of the three. I do not know whether you are going to act on my advice, but I hope you will do so.

Sommy then read out the pedigree of Sceptre, digressing to comment on the merits of her sire Persimmon before asking for an opening bid of 5000 guineas.

People seldom enjoy being preached at, and although they were more tolerant of this sort of didactic and repetitive flannel in 1911 than they are inclined to be in the last quarter of the century, the effects of Sommy's lecture seem to have been at best soporific. The bidding stuck at 6800 guineas. After a lengthy pause he announced a bid of 7000 guineas and, when no further rise was forthcoming, the hammer fell and he stated that Messrs Tattersall were the purchasers. The announcement was greeted by polite applause.

Sceptre became the property of Sommy himself and bred him two small winners, but changed hands three more times before she died at the age of twenty-seven. What emerges from the story of her 1911 sale is that Sommy's long and tedious introductory address, far from heightening the sense of drama at a great occasion, actually lowered it by inducing feelings of lethargy and boredom in the audience.

The dramatic temperature was very different at the sale of

Vaguely Noble, who realized the record price of 136,000 guineas as a two-year-old at the December Sales in 1967. He won the Prix de L'Arc de Triomphe the next year

Vaguely Noble on 7 December 1967. Vaguely Noble was submitted as one of a batch of sixteen horses-in-training owned by the executors of the late Major Lionel Holliday, who had died two years earlier. Holliday had set himself exacting standards of soundness, speed and Classic ability as one of the most successful English breeders, and had won Classic races with Night Off, Neasham Belle and Hethersett during the last fifteen years of his life. When Vaguely Noble came up for sale he was two years old and had given unmistakable signs of developing into the best horse Holliday had ever bred. During the autumn he had won the Sandwich Stakes at Ascot by 12 lengths and the Observer Gold Cup (later the Group 1 William Hill Futurity) at Doncaster by 7 lengths, and had been allotted second place in the Free Handicap with only 1lb less than the brilliant Petingo. No two-year-old of such high class and exciting prospects as a middle-distance performer had ever been presented in an English sale ring.

As 6.00 p.m., the hour at which Vaguely Noble was due to be sold, approached, the new sales pavilion, which had been in use for only two years, began to fill up steadily. Expectancy was running high and there was a buzz of animated conversation. By the time that Nocturne, the lot immediately preceding Vaguely Noble, was knocked down to the Italian Dr Carlo Vittadini for 2200 guineas the building was filled far beyond its estimated capacity, and spectators were packed solid in the aisles and in the doorways and corridors through which the horses had to enter and leave the ring. A hush fell as Ken Watt, the auctioneer conducting the sale, began his introductory remarks:

One thousand and forty-four [Vaguely Noble's catalogue number] – Vaguely Noble, a two-year-old bay colt by Vienna out of Noble Lassie by Nearco. You know as much about him as I do, gentlemen. He's won two races very, very easily, the Sandwich Stakes at Ascot and the Observer Gold Cup at Doncaster. Now this horse is a rarity to be offered at auction. He's second in the Free Handicap and a good-looking hardy colt of great scope on clean limbs and typical of the Holliday breed.

At this point Watt had to pause because of a commotion in the entrance corridor. A crowd of people had swarmed through the doors in the wake of Vaguely Noble and were surging forward in their attempts to obtain vantage points, pressing those in front of them against the retaining rope at the edge of the ring. 'Let 'em back please, let 'em back,' Watt called out. George Forbes, the bloodstock agent, who was in his habitual position on the rope, appeared to be in danger of being cut in half. He was a powerful man, but he was in trouble. 'This is ridiculous in this ring – and someone will get hurt,' Watt admonished. At last order was restored and the sale was able to proceed.

Watt announced immediately that he was bid 80,000 guineas, nearly double the existing Tattersalls record price realized by Solario thirty-five years earlier. The bidding advanced rapidly to 100,000, at which point the BBA dropped out. There was no real check until 120,000 when Watt commented: 'He's dual purpose, you know.' Captain Tim Rogers ventured 125,000. Another pause followed, and Watt made his next comment: 'He could still be cheap.' Albert Yank, of the World Wide Bloodstock Agency, bid 130,000. It was becoming harder to extract the bids. At last the French agent Godolphin Darley, representing the Texas oil magnate Bunker Hunt, signalled a bid. '135,000?' queried Watt, and then, as Godolphin Darley raised one finger, '131,000, yes certainly.' The bidding rose by 1000 guineas at a time to 134,000, at which figure Godolphin Darley again hesitated. 'Now don't get beat', Watt encouraged him, and he responded by bidding 135,000. Yank bid 136,000. This time Godolphin Darley and Hunt were ready to quit. 'Are you quite sure now? For this outstanding colt?' said Watt. But there was no further bidding, and Vaguely Noble was knocked down to the World Wide Bloodstock Agency.

The announcement of the result of the sale caused something like consternation, because few in the audience had even heard of the World Wide Bloodstock Agency. Yank, a short swarthy man, was besieged by members of the Press eager to get the story. It transpired that Yank had bought the colt for Dr Robert Franklyn, a plastic surgeon from California whose special skill was said to lie in 'making the beautiful ladies of Hollywood even more beautiful'. Vaguely Noble was sent to Paddy Prendergast's stable at the Curragh. However, Bunker Hunt was not a man to take defeat lying down when such a choice lot was involved. He quickly entered into negotiations, and early in 1968 completed a deal to buy a half-share in Vaguely Noble, who was transferred to Etienne Pollet's stable at Chantilly.

There is always an element of a gamble in paying record prices for thoroughbreds. In the case of Vaguely Noble the gambling element was even more pronounced than usual, because he had been omitted for the Classic races for which in those days horses had to be entered in February of their two-year-old season, and his sire Vienna was not universally esteemed. The only way in which Vaguely Noble could maintain or enhance his value was to beat the best of the Classic horses in the Prix de l'Arc de Triomphe, the great French international race in October. With this exclusive target in view, it made sense that he should be trained by Pollet, a master of the art of training middle-distance horses who was perfectly placed to take advantage of the excellent French programme of races leading up the 'Arc'. This ambitious plan succeeded to a degree that only a consummate optimist would have dared hope when Vaguely Noble beat the Derby winner Sir Ivor decisively in the 'Arc', and then retired

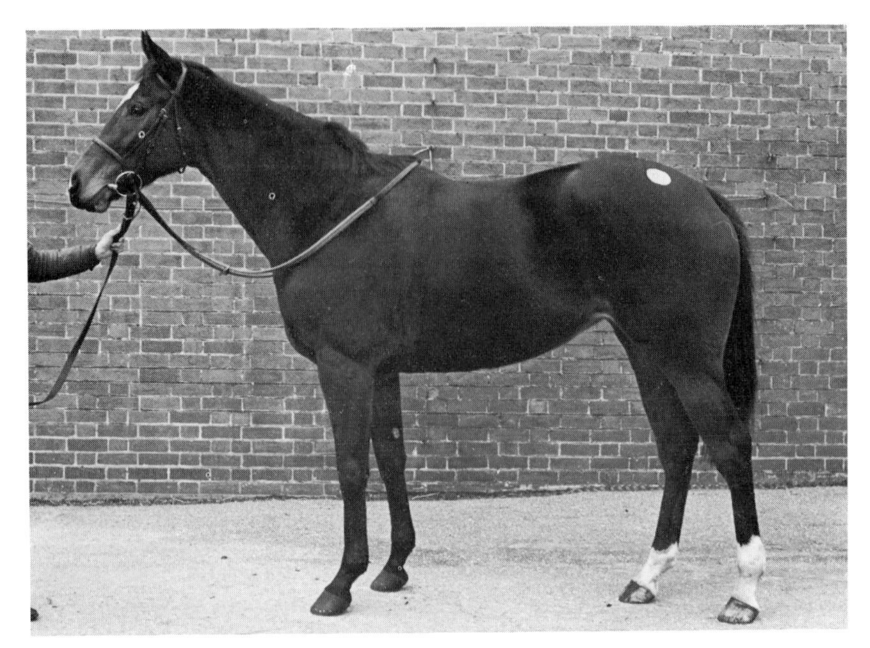

Tenea (by Reform out of Stilvi) – she made auctioneering history as the first British sales 'millionaire' when she realized 1,020,000 guineas as a three-year-old at the Newmarket December Sales in 1982

to stud in Kentucky to become one of the leading Classic stallions of his day, with the 1976 Derby winner Empery, owned and bred by Bunker Hunt, among his progeny. The events in the sale ring of the Park Paddocks on that December evening of 1967 had been only a single act of one of the great dramas of thoroughbred history.

Another of the dramas played before a well-filled house was that involving Britain's first auction 'millionaire', Tenea, at the 1982 December Sales, though the Tenea sale was of a different order from that of Vaguely Noble because the tension and excitement owed comparatively little to anticipation but built up progressively as the bidding rose unexpectedly to record levels. Tenea was a three-year-old filly by Reform out of Stilvi, one of the most outstanding successful broodmares of the time. Stilvi herself had been fast, winning four Pattern races over 5 and 6 furlongs at two and three years old. She transmitted her speed to most of her offspring in generous measure, and by the time Tenea was sold she had been responsible for four performers of the highest class in the Irish Sweeps Derby winner Tyrnavos, the Group 1 William

Hill Dewhurst Stakes winner Tromos, and Tachypous and Tolmi, who were second in the 2000 and the 1000 Guineas respectively.

Tenea showed nothing like the same racing class. She finished sixth in a race at Doncaster at two years old, and never ran again owing to an accident. Consequently she was difficult to value. Bruce Hobbs had trained Stilvi and all her successful offspring for the Greek shipowner George Cambanis, and also acted as racing manager for the Cambanis family. Tenea was owned by George Cambanis's widow. When Hobbs telephoned to discuss the reserve price that should be put on Tenea with Richard Mildmay-White, the Tattersalls director who was to sell her, Mildmay-White expressed the opinion that she should make £250,000. 'Then you think it should be safe to put on a reserve of 50,000 guineas?' asked Hobbs; and that figure was agreed. In the event, when Tenea entered the ring at 5.50 p.m. on 30 November the bidding opened at the reserve price. Most of the early running was made by the Newmarket trainer Tom Jones and the Houston newspaper publisher Joe Allbritton, until the previous filly record of 420,000 guineas, set up by Northern Valley the previous year, was passed. At that point Jones dropped out, but Sir Philip Payne-Gallwey of the BBA immediately joined in. The next target was 730,000, the record price for any category of bloodstock set up by the five-year-old mare Greenland Park at the 1981 December Sales (incidentally Greenland Park had been a top-class two-year-old and sprinter and was in foal to the much sought-after young stallion Kris). About this stage the bidding became sluggish, and Mildmay-White thought the end was near. Suddenly, however, the bidding came alive again. 'When that happened,' Mildmay-White said later, 'I felt sure it would reach a million, because there was no logical stopping place before we got there.'

People were pouring in as they became aware of what was going on, and the arena was packed by the time Payne-Gallwey finally bid the million. Albritton made one more bid, but when Payne-Gallwey capped it immediately with a bid of 1,020,000 guineas Albritton was silenced, and Mildmay-White brought down the hammer in favour of Payne-Gallwey. The filly had been bought for the Greek shipowner Stavros Niarchos and Robert Sangster; the two men already owned a number of horses in partnership. The new record had outrun the advance of Tattersalls into the technological age: the electronic bid indicator had reached its limit at 999,990 guineas.

If Sommy Tattersall tended to prolixity in comparison with his successors, he also imposed the most daunting tests of stamina upon himself as an auctioneer. He thought nothing of selling on his own for a whole day, and even for several days on end, at the bigger sales. It is true that he had the relief of meal breaks, whereas continuous day-long selling became the rule in the second half of the twentieth century. Selling at the December Sales in 1900 was at the rate of 80 horses a day, whereas it was at the rate of 131 a day, an increase of 64%, in 1985; moreover the December Sales lasted no more than six days in 1900, but lasted eleven days in 1985. Nevertheless the sheer physical strain of selling even at the 1900 rate must have been extremely taxing, and occasional lapses of concentration must surely have been inevitable.

Ken Watt became convinced that selling even for a period of an hour tired the larynx, and that selling for longer periods was bound to result in impaired standards of performance. He introduced the system of employing eight or nine auctioneers at the bigger sales and using them in short, sharp bursts of about ten lots, though the actual number of lots sold in individual sessions may range from eight to fifteen lots. 'When I first came to the firm,' he recalled, 'selling was based on twenty lots a time and the speed was very much slower. My introduction to auctioneering was the result of an order from Bob Needham that I was to sell 22 lots at 11.30 the next day.' The work rate in the 1940s was a kind of mean between the marathon stints of Sommy Tattersall's early days and the modern system. Nevertheless this transition did not tell the whole story. While the modern system may impose less strain on individual auctioneers, Tattersalls recognized the importance of proper voice control not only to ensure clarity of diction and consequently accurate communication with bidders, but also to reduce fatigue during the longer sales. For this reason it has been the firm's practice for staff auctioneers and newly joined members of the firm lacking previous auctioneering experience to receive instruction at the Central School of Speech and Drama (later RADA) – a thoroughly appropriate source of training in view of the kinship between the rostrum and the stage.

To switch from a theatrical to a sporting analogy, Ken believed in frequent changes of bowling. Frequent changes kept the auctioneers fresh, and prevented onlookers from getting bored or simply drifting away. An alert and interested audience may always include a few who find themselves bidding without premeditation. Onlookers are kept on their toes by the contrasts between the classical British auctioneering styles of Ken Watt, Michael Watt and Richard Mildmay-White, the histrionic gestures and sense of urgency generated by Sir Peter Nugent and the bit of the blarney and the entertaining asides dispensed by David Pim. Pim, a Tattersalls (Ireland) staff auctioneer who sells regularly at Newmarket, has a gift for making apt and amusing comments which introduce light relief into the serious business of buying and selling, as at the 1985 December Sales when he described the horse he was selling as 'the best walker you've ever seen since Ian Botham' – a topical reference to the England all-rounder's recently completed charity walk from John-o'-Groats to Land's End. All the auctioneers take their turns at selling good horses, though the very choicest may be allotted to the most experienced. For example, it was no coincidence that Vaguely Noble was sold by Ken Watt, the chairman and senior auctioneer at the time.

Tattersalls sales have a disarmingly informal air, with ample scope for the auctioneer to express and project his personality, compared with the stereotyped American bloodstock sales which are characterized by the monotonous chant derived from the old tobacco auctions and by the intervention of the spotters who actually take the bids. At Keeneland, for example, the bidder may not even be visible to the auctioneer as he may be positioned in the collecting area at the back of the rostrum and outside the main sales pavilion. In the 1980s Tattersalls reinforced their rostrum team of spotters with spotters dispersed round the ring. These outlying spotters were attractive girls whose effect on the whole scene was undoubtedly decorative as well as useful; but in the Park Paddocks the function of spotters is purely to draw the attention of the auctioneer to a bidder he may have missed, never to accept a bid. At the principal American sales the dinner jackets of the auctioneers, the uniforms of the spotters and the fact that the horse being sold is held stationary on a platform below the rostrum combine to create an atmosphere of formality which is not in evidence at Newmarket.

It has never been Tattersalls' contention that their methods of conducting bloodstock sales are superior to the American, except in so far as the bidder has a better chance of judging the athletic capacity of a horse being led round a spacious oval ring than a horse standing still. They have been insistent that their methods have evolved in step with British traditions and requirements and are most suitable for British conditions. It is unthinkable that the Watts should employ the chant. However, informality in the Park Paddocks is not complete, because paradoxically the auctioneers and their male spotters do adopt what may be described as a kind of country casual uniform, consisting of tweed hacking jacket, cavalry twill or grey worsted trousers, woollen pullover, shirt of not too assertive check pattern and tie of sober hue. They look more like stud managers or landowners than members of the so-called 'professional classes'.

This diffidence of Tattersalls was not shared by Tony Morris, whose preference for the British style of auctioneering was pungently expressed in his *Racing Post* article. He wrote:

Consider for a moment the way we do the job in this country. The auctioneer, in sole charge of the proceedings, introduces the horse briefly, asks for an offer and calls the bids. The fellow who can count can get by, but the real art is displayed by those who know their bidders and how to motivate them to compete.

In America the system is totally different, and they go through a loud and spectacular ritual of fuss and bluster to compensate for the loss of art.

The auctioneer saves his voice while an announcer introduces the horses with lengthy background detail everyone already knows. Then the chanting begins, the auctioneer calling for the bid he wants, and responding rapidly to the hollers of frenetic bid spotters who urge and cajole the victims in their area into action. Make no mistake, there is a deal of skill involved. But it is evident only in the pressure tactics of those hyper-active spotters, some of whom leap around, wave their arms and scream like demented pop fans. The auctioneer is frequently unaware of the identities of the bidders, his only tenuous contact being through the spotters. The overall effect of this rowdy and raucous behaviour can be to generate excitement in the auditorium, but when the market is less than buoyant it all smacks of much ado about nothing.

Despite the variety and individuality of the British style, there are certain conventional phrases which recur regularly in the patter of Tattersalls auctioneers: for example, 'I can't dwell', 'quick as you bid', 'I'm giving him away', and 'have you quite done?' – all designed to galvanize hesitant bidders; and 'in the gate', 'on the stairs', 'opposite', 'under the window', 'in front', 'behind' and similar descriptions to indicate the positions of bidders around the ring. 'In front' and 'behind' can be vitally important when two people bidding for the same lot are directly in the same line of sight from the auctioneer. There have been occasional misunderstandings when the auctioneer has failed to convince one of a pair of bidders that his rival made the last bid. In those circumstances it is essential for the auctioneer to take extreme pains to communicate the true state of the bidding to each of the rivals. In extreme cases, Ken Watt recalled, he had found it necessary to mention one of the bidders by name, although this is contrary to normal practice.

It is the duty of the auctioneer to obtain the best possible price for the vendor. For this purpose he must bring to the attention of bidders any points that may be made in favour of the horse currently under the hammer; but at the same time he must tell the truth. Thus it may be perfectly fair and accurate to speak of 'a good topped filly' when she has a twisted leg, and equally fair and accurate to speak of a colt's 'good clean limbs' when he has a common head and a dip in his back. Within reason, in auctioneering sins of omission count only in respect of faults listed in the conditions of sale, such as wind-sucking, whistling and roaring. In the early days of Tattersalls the legitimate practice of drawing attention to a horse's good points was known as 'puffing' or 'chaunting', though at some places other than Hyde Park Corner the convention was certainly abused. Surtees had this to say of the more extreme forms of 'chaunting' in his book *The Horseman's Manual*, published in 1831:

> Auctioneers have long been the privileged dealers in flowery metaphors and exaggerated descriptions, but the thing is now carried to such a height as to call loudly for the interference of the Legislature.
>
> We have all heard of the advertisements of an estate for sale commanding an extensive view over hill and dale, having the

landscape varied by a beautiful 'hanging wood' and which, on the purchaser's taking possession of the house, proved to be a gallows.

Such verbal excesses were eliminated from auctioneering long ago, and modern 'chaunting' at bloodstock sales is essentially discreet, strictly truthful and free from misleading ambiguities.

This concept of the way an auction house should conduct its business conforms strictly to the moral principles on which the first Richard Tattersall founded the firm. Ken Watt, as quoted by Janelle Harding in *The Thoroughbred Record*, summed up those principles in these words: 'He [Richard Tattersall] founded the firm on pure honesty and straight dealing, which isn't always known among horse people. I think that's why we've gone on for more than two centuries. We never, ever try to do anything that is just to our advantage, but not quite straight. People know that.'

Over the whole range of their policies Tattersalls have adopted a kind of progressive conservatism, striving to keep true to their best traditions while taking pride in being leaders in technological innovation whenever technology can improve efficiency. For example, the indicator boards in the Glasgow Paddocks and the Park Paddocks before rebuilding resembled nothing so much as the score-board at a village cricket ground. But by 1985 the main indicator board was an electronic marvel displaying the latest bids not only in sterling – no more limit at 999,990 guineas – but also converted into the equivalent in all the major international currencies.

Nor does technology represent the only kind of change that has affected Tattersalls' working practices. The introduction of select sales and the transfer of responsibility for selection and the allocation of each yearling to its appropriate sale – Highflyer and the October Sales – involves a tremendous amount of work in the field. In the middle 1980s this involved the inspection of more than 1500 yearlings, and for this purpose their parent studs were divided into areas – the south, the north, Newmarket, the Midlands and the north-west of England, Ireland and the Continent of Europe – each with its team of inspecting auctioneers. With the need to revisit a number of studs to monitor the progress of immature, sick or injured yearlings, the inspection process occupied most of the months of May and June.

The busy scene at the October yearling sales

The summer tour did not absolve the auctioneers from the need to see the yearlings after their arrival at the Park Paddocks. For one thing, the yearlings allotted to each auctioneer to sell might not be the same that he had inspected; for another, the yearlings allotted to him might have developed unpredictably in the intervening months even if he had inspected them; and for another thing again, it was essential for the auctioneer to have the latest possible picture of each yearling in his mind's eye in order to describe it accurately on entry into the ring and to enable him to give authentic advice on the subject of a reserve price.

Obviously these intricacies of the auctioneer's craft call for a high degree of dedication and professionalism to retain the confidence of buyers and sellers. Although many vendors make requests for specific auctioneers and Tattersalls have tried to oblige them as far as possible without showing favouritism, it has never been possible to meet everyone's first choice, and the alternative must be a person of demonstrable competence.

But if it is the duty of Tattersalls to obtain the best price possible for the vendor, it is also the function of Tattersalls to hold the ring fairly between vendor and buyer. Surtees described sales by public auction as places where 'the doctrine of "*caveat emptor*" – "let the buyer beware" – well applied.' In modern times that doctrine has been circumscribed and contracted by many rights and conditions that help to protect the buyer. The racing authorities have introduced increasingly strict measures of identification of thoroughbreds, and the equine passports have to be lodged with Tattersalls before sale. In the case of broodmares, those described as 'believed in foal' must have a covering certificate deposited with Tattersalls. The Conditions of Sale embrace strict regulations concerning the sale of wind-suckers, whistlers and roarers, which are returnable unless so described. A whistler and/or roarer is defined as 'a horse which can be heard to make a characteristic abnormal inspiratory sound when actively exercised'. Facilities for inspection on the endoscope were provided at the Park Paddocks. There is ample room in the various stable yards for inspection by potential buyers of horses outside their boxes. Altogether there is little force left in the words written by Surtees a century and a half ago:

> I believe it is generally allowed by persons conversant with horse-dealing, that those who know nothing about horses, if they must purchase their knowledge, had better purchase it at the cheapest rate; and that sales by private contract, where a reasonable trial is allowed, afford much better opportunities of becoming acquainted with the necessary requisites for a good horse, than those by public auction, where the place of trial and inspection is a small and crowded yard.

6
Tattersalls Men

APART from all his other virtues which contributed to the progress of Tattersalls' business in the first half of the twentieth century, Sommy Tattersall had an exceptionally sure instinct for the selection of men with the right qualities to serve the interests of the firm. Two of the men that he brought in, Gerald Deane and Terry Watt, not only proved excellent auctioneers and partners – though Terry Watt's tenure of office was regrettably brief – but themselves had sons who in due course joined the firm and helped to provide the continuity which was an invaluable factor in further expansion during the second half of the century. Once Terry had been recruited, of course, there was only a short time – between his death and the advent of his first cousin Ken – when there was no member of the Watt family in the firm.

Terry Watt's son Michael and Gerald Deane's son Bruce are practically the same age, as they were both born in 1933, and joined the firm within 6 months of each other in 1954. Michael was appointed a partner three years later and became chairman on the retirement of Ken at the end of 1982, and Bruce became a partner in 1964 and a director when the status of the firm was changed to that of a private limited company the same year.

Michael Watt was educated at Eton and afterwards joined his father's old regiment, the Life Guards, as a National Service officer, serving for two years. However, the 1950s were a period fraught with problems for Tattersalls as Ken Watt struggled to restore the position after the sudden death of Bob Needham and the long mental illness and eventual death of Gerald Deane, and Ken used all his powers of persuasion to induce Michael to join the firm as soon as possible. Michael acquiesced, but showed his independent spirit by refusing to be hurried. He took hunting leave for the winter of 1953–4, and joined the firm in April of the latter year – his arrival practically coinciding with his twenty-first birthday.

Michael's first employment at the sales was as a spotter, an experience which taught him that the prompt and accurate spotting of bids is a difficult art which must be picked up gradually. At the same time he was attending the Central School of Speech and Drama in Queen's Gate to learn to breathe properly and reduce the strain on throat and larynx when auctioneering. The first important occasion on which he sold horses was the Dewar dispersal at the end of 1954, when the almost priceless collection of fillies and mares attracted exceptionally animated bidding and lifted the December Sales aggregate above the million-guineas mark for the first time.

Michael quickly became a first-class auctioneer. He was very like his father. Facially the resemblance was uncannily close and was accentuated by the fact that they wore similar dark-rimmed glasses. Their tones of voice were the same. Michael's aunt Cecil McCullough summed up the likeness: 'Now when I come to Newmarket and Michael Watt stands up and sells horses I see and hear so many things that are Terry all over again.' One of his greatest assets as an auctioneer is perfect clarity of enunciation. Only the stone-deaf can fail to hear and understand every syllable he utters.

Nevertheless Michael Watt is no mere carbon copy of his father. He is a man of strong will, incisive in judgement, intolerant of folly and inefficiency wherever he finds those faults, and armed with a swift and penetrating wit and shrewd judgement of character. His resilience after he had sustained severe internal injuries in a hunting fall was typical of his defiant attitude to adversity. He had to undergo a major operation and was away from Tattersalls for 6 months, but fought his way back to a state of almost full health in which his capacity for work was certainly undiminished and he was once again able to enjoy his favourite recreations of hunting, shooting and tennis.

Although a man with a definite mind of his own on most matters, he is prepared to delegate authority and defer to the judgement of people whose opinion he trusts. He had absolute confidence in Jack Knight, who was Tattersalls' accountant in the 1950s and ran the financial affairs of the firm practically on his own. Michael remarks admiringly of him: 'When I joined the firm I quickly learnt to have complete faith in Jack Knight and sign any cheques he put in front of me without question. He had the marvellous faculty of knowing a bad risk at once when a man came into the office wanting credit.'

It is more than possible that future historians of bloodstock auctioneering will recognize Michael's distinctive contribution to the evolution of Tattersalls as his constant drive to keep pace – and indeed a step ahead of rival auction houses – with the development of the international market in thoroughbreds while preserving the firm's traditional values. His outward-looking stance found graphic expression in his 'Chairman's Message' published in the initial *Tatteralls Newsletter* in the spring of 1985. Looking ahead to the year's activities he wrote:

The Directors will as usual be out on tour; after a brief visit to Miami for a Society of International Thoroughbred Auctioneers meeting, I hope to be in South Africa in March for their sales with David Pim of Ballsbridge-Tattersalls, before returning to Europe for my usual visit to French and German clients, following last year's successful Swedish trip. Richard Mildmay-White will be going to Australasia and Hong Kong. Ken Watt, Peter Nugent and Edmond Mahony will soon be on the road in Ireland, visiting clients old and new. On the American front, Bruce Deane and David Stoddart will attend the main Kentucky Sales and Tattersalls will be sponsoring a high handicap polo match at Saratoga during the sales and race meeting there in August.

Tattersalls have resident representatives in some of the most important thoroughbred racing and breeding countries: for example, John Palmer in Australia and Linda Conley in the United States. However, in respect of international contacts Michael Watt leads from the front. Apart from his occasional visits to more distant markets like the United States, South America and South Africa, he is a regular visitor to France and Germany to inspect yearlings, maintain and increase contacts and advise when requested. In 1986 he began to assist with the selection process for the main German yearling sales at Baden-Baden. His outward-looking attitude, was clearly expressed in a letter to David Gibson, then chairman of the council of the Thoroughbred Breeders Association, in October 1985:

Tattersalls regard themselves as International Bloodstock Auctioneers, serving most parts of the world. We sell horses to between forty-five and fifty different countries and horses from America,

England and Ireland, and all the Continent of Europe, come here to be sold. We have long and traditional links with Ireland and it has been a most valuable connection on both sides, going back as far as the start of the Doncaster Yearling Sales in the last century.

His international outlook is exemplified by his chairmanship of the Society of International Thoroughbred Auctioneers (SITA) formed by six of the leading auction houses of the Northern Hemisphere in 1983, for the main purpose of creating a forum for the discussion of mutual problems.

Michael married Susan, the only daughter of Major Leigh Ingham Tomkins Whitaker, of Bordon in Hampshire, on 7 November 1959. His father-in-law became High Sheriff of Hampshire three years later. There were four children, two daughters and two sons, of the marriage. After the death of his first wife, Michael married Mrs Marjorie Johnson from Cheshire. They live at Greens Park, Towcester, in Northamptonshire.

Bruce Deane's road to a directorship was very different from that of Michael Watt. He was sent as an evacuee to Canada early in the Second World War and on his return home 5 years later at the age of twelve was found, like many another evacuee, to have learnt little – educationally speaking – during his time abroad. He went to a crammer and passed into Tonbridge School, but his career there was undistinguished and he left at the age of sixteen. The idea was that he should do one year of practical farming work and one year of study of the theory of agriculture, but his father died after the first year and the responsibility for the family stud farm and property at Littleton became his.

Bruce was called up for National Service in 1952. He had hoped to join the Royal Greenjackets, whose depot was at Winchester almost within sight of his home, but he failed the medical test on account of his chronic asthma. Instead he was drafted into the Royal Army Veterinary Corps and spent most of his two years' service in the Orderly Room at the depot at Melton Mowbray. It was not an exciting or inspiring kind of military service, but Bruce did consider that he derived one real benefit from it. That was to be a good social mixer, as his father had been before him, and that is an important asset for a member of an auction house who must meet and have harmonious relations with member of all classes, all professions and many different nationalities.

Bruce joined Tattersalls in September 1954, but his first seven years in the firm were fraught with personal problems. He became ill with TB in August 1955 and was away from work for nearly a year. Then in January 1960 he suffered serious injuries, including a broken leg, in a car accident, and had only reached the convalescent stage when he slipped at London Airport and broke the same leg again. He was unable to return to the office until May 1961. He was a sufferer from hay fever from childhood. Asthma supervened, and troubles him every summer from haymaking onwards.

Although Bruce did his share of auctioneering for many years, his main contribution to the progress of Tattersalls has not been on the rostrum. Exceptionally hard-working and conscientious, he has overall responsibility for the administ-ration of the Park Paddocks and the box-building programme, and for dealing with suppliers, tradesmen and printers. He plays a full part in the inspection and selection of yearlings for the Highflyer Sales, generally touring the studs in the South of England in company with Peter Holmes. He also makes frequent visits to the United States, where he tours as many stud farms as possible with Andrew Howland, and also Linda Conley, who is Tattersalls' resident representative.

Bruce is convinced that it is possible to make much more useful personal contacts on the stud farms than at the sales, where breeders tend to be preoccupied with the business of buying and selling. Breeders are more relaxed away from the hectic atmosphere of Keeneland or Saratoga, and on the farm it is possible to get to know and understand their backgrounds and personalities, and the kind of bloodstock in which they may specialize. All the information so gleaned is likely to be invaluable, whether the breeders concerned be actual or merely potential clients of Tattersalls.

On stud tours, in either of his roles of inspector and ambassador, he has the advantage of the intimate knowledge of breeding thoroughbreds and its problems which comes from the fact that he is a successful breeder himself. Although Littleton, which he inherited, had been a thriving stud in the period between the wars, its fortunes had declined and there was a doubt whether Bruce would be able to carry on after his father died. 'Then we had the good fortune to get hold of Vilmorin as a stallion in 1955, and after that we were able to pay our way', recalls Bruce. Vilmorin had been a top-class sprinter, winning the King's Stand Stakes at Royal Ascot, and was a leading sire of fast and precocious horses; consequently his services were always in strong demand. Vilmorin died in 1963 at the age of twenty. At the December Sales the following year Bruce was able to buy his best son Quorum, who had been second to the mighty Crepello in the 2000 Guineas, cheaply for 10,500 guineas, though he had feared that the horse might realize double that price. Quorum was then ten years old and was as great an asset to Littleton as his sire had been. Quorum was succeeded by another very fast horse, Song, whose stud career also was distinguished by a capacity to transmit his great speed, in spite of interruptions, both for health reasons and because he once broke a leg.

Bruce Deane has had some notable successes as a breeder as well as a stallion manager. The most brilliant of his produce was Devon Ditty, by the home stallion Song, who was sold for 7800 guineas at the Houghton Sales in 1977 and proceeded to win four Pattern races, including the two-year-old fillies' championship race, the Cheveley Park Stakes, the next year. Six years later he sold a colt by Homing for 36,000 guineas at the Highflyer Sales. Named Don Orazio, this colt gave Bruce his first Classic victory as breeder when he won the Italian Derby in 1985.

Bruce sold Littleton in 1984, but this did not mean the end of his breeding operations. He built a new stud on 50 acres of virgin stud-farming land on the south-facing slopes of Bishop's Down near Bishop's Waltham, 10 miles south-east of Winchester. There are no stallions at Bishop's Down, and Bruce has concentrated on assembling a small but select band of mares to produce for the yearling market. The investment is considerable. For example, Bruce bought the young Green Dancer mare Very Nice, in foal to Posse, for no less than 175,000 guineas at the December Sales in 1984. He is a supporter of his own firm as both buyer and seller.

As an active breeder himself, Bruce Deane has been an appropriate representative of Tattersalls on the Council of the Thoroughbred Breeders Association for many years. The presence of a Tattersalls representative gives the Council an important liaison function and makes it a forum for exchanges of views between Tattersalls and many of the breeders who are among the firm's principal clients. Bruce is also Tattersalls' representative on the International Cataloguing Standards Committee, which has a close affiliation with SITA. The Committee's brochure for 1986 described its work in these terms:

> In the four years since its formation, the International Cataloguing Standards Committee has worked to achieve uniformity of cataloguing standards throughout the world in a time of increasing internationalism in Thoroughbred breeding, racing and marketing. The committee is made up of representatives of the racing authorities, breeders organizations, and international auction houses of four major breeding and racing countries [England, France, Ireland and the United States].

There is no doubt that Bruce's equable and dignified demeanour, his imperturbable good manners, his careful attention to detail and his constant refusal to be stampeded into facile and ill-considered solutions to complex problems have served the TBA, the ICSC and Tattersalls well. He personifies the common-sense maxim: 'Hasten slowly' – which has, indeed, governed and guided the evolution of Tattersalls in the second half of the twentieth century.

Richard Mildmay-White, who was born in 1949, is the youngest of the Tattersalls directors but the next to be appointed to the board after Bruce Deane. He has close family connections both with the larger world of racing and with the present chairman of Tattersalls, because he was a nephew of the former leading and much-loved amateur rider Lord Mildmay, while his mother and Michael Watt's mother were first cousins. To cement the relationship, Anthony and Helen Mildmay were Michael's godparents.

Lord Mildmay, known generally in the racing community as Anthony Mildmay, was leading amateur four times by a clear margin and tied once with Bobby Petre for the lead between the 1937/8 and the 1949/50 National Hunt seasons. The surest way of imprinting your name indelibly in the annals of the Turf is by a spectacular failure, and Anthony Mildmay is remembered better for the tragi-comedy of the 1936 Grand National, when his mount Davy Jones ran out at the last fence with the race at his mercy, because the reins had broken, than for any one of his 197 victories. He never did win the Grand National, though he was third on his own horse Cromwell a dozen years after the Davy Jones disaster.

Anthony Mildmay's death by drowning while swimming off the Devon coast on 12 May 1950 was pure tragedy. He was just forty-one years old and, even if he had not continued to ride in races a great deal longer, he would certainly have given many years of service to racing as an administrator and member of the National Hunt Committee. His sportsmanship, his fortitude and his determination earned the respect and affection of everyone in racing. His success as a race-rider was all the more remarkable because he was not the right shape for a jockey, being far too tall, and was not a natural horseman. In his early days of race-riding, often at west country meetings, old stagers were apt to scoff at his long thin form and his loose seat in the saddle. Sheer perseverance and an indomitable will to overcome his inherent disadvantages made him the highly effective race-rider that he eventually became.

This digression may be excused because Richard Mildmay-White – his father, John White, who married Anthony's sister Helen, added 'Mildmay' to his own surname because the male line of the Mildmays was extinct – resembles his uncle in some significant respects. Richard has the same lean face and features, and he too is tall. Richard also has some of his uncle's sterling character. Although he did not have the same success as a race-rider, he rode in point-to-points and hunter chases. His proudest moment on the racecourse was on 15 April 1974 at Fairyhouse, when he won the T. Levins-Moore Memorial Hunters Chase on Lovely Job an hour after Colebridge had beaten that great chaser L'Escargot, winner of the Cheltenham Gold Cup and the Grand National, in the Irish Grand National. However, dreams of glory as an amateur jockey were destroyed when a bad fall and a broken vertebra in his neck forced him to give up race-riding.

His first move on recovering from his injuries was to spend some time with Alan Lillingston at Mount Coote in County Limerick, where the atmosphere and glamour of a top-class stud whetted his appetite for involvement in racing. He next went to Cirencester to study agriculture and estate management, but the decision of his elder brother Anthony, later a Steward of the Jockey Club, to return to Devon and run the family estate left him at a loose end. At this point his mother approached Michael Watt to ask whether there might be an opening for him with Tattersalls, but received no encouragement. To fill in time while trying to find a suitable career,

Richard went out to Australia and worked as a gardener, making enough money to go round the principal sales and race meetings. Meanwhile Michael Watt had second thoughts, and sent out a summons to him to join the firm. So he was in, after all; but the time in Australia had not been wasted, because he had made many friends and contacts that were to prove useful in the future.

Richard Mildmay-White joined Tattersalls in 1972, when he was twenty-three years old, and became a director three years later. Like some of his colleagues, he took elocution lessons before he began to sell horses, but expresses some scepticism as to their value because the acoustic system of the Park Paddocks sales building, with loudspeakers attached to the backs of the seats, absolves the auctioneers from the necessity of 'throwing' their voices. However, he does concede that the lessons may have served a purpose by teaching him to conserve his breath.

Whether the elocution lessons were useful or not, Richard became an extremely good auctioneer, as no less an authority than Ken Watt has testified. Richard's rostrum style clearly owes much to the models of the Watt cousins, and he uses many of the phrases that they have put into auctioneering currency. If Ken Watt admires him as an auctioneer, then their respect is mutual. Ken was chairman when he joined the firm, and Richard has said of him:

> Ken was a wonderful man to work with. He led, but did not lay down the law. He liked people to express their own opinions and disagree with him if necessary.

Richard admits that Tattersalls still had a rather fusty image in the early 1970s, but all that changed when Goffs opened their Kill sales complex and emerged as an important international auction house in the middle of that decade. He believes in the spur of healthy competition. He is convinced that the pre-eminence of Tattersalls depends on the firm's reputation for getting the best possible price for every lot. Although the big sales like that of Tenea may catch the headlines, just as much effort must be put into extracting a bid of 10,000 guineas for a horse that has been hanging fire around 5000 guineas, because the difference really matters to the small breeder.

One of Richard's special responsibilities is sifting the pedigrees of all the horses entered for the yearling sales before the annual round of inspection visits begins in May. With 1630 yearlings entered in 1985 and 1750 in 1986, the winnowing process involves several weeks of concentrated hard work. In respect of Michael Watt's policy of maintaining and strengthening foreign contacts by directors travelling abroad during the close season for Tattersalls sales, Australia is naturally Richard's patch. Richard believes in the usefulness of these visits, but is cautious in assessing the benefits in precise trading terms. He explains:

To go out there and try to press Australians to buy British bloodstock would not be very effective. Australian buying depends on many imponderable factors like the tax position, the state of the Australian economy and the exchange rate, and the requirements of individual breeders. There is only a limited amount of persuasion I can do. In any case, we have our resident representative John Palmer who understands local conditions much better. But the contacts I make certainly are helpful when Australians come to England and the sales, because Newmarket can be an intimidating place to anyone who does not know it well. It is good for the visitors to feel that they have a friend to turn to. We can help in lots of ways like hotel bookings through our Public Relations secretary, Lavinia Thompson.

Richard Mildmay-White is undoubtedly a key member of the Tattersalls team. His family background and upbringing gave him an almost instinctive feeling for horses; and if his accident put a premature end to his race-riding, he has remained very much a hunting man, keeping two horses in the Quorn country during the season.

The one remaining director, Sir Peter Nugent, Bt, is considerably older than Richard Mildmay-White, having been born in 1920. Peter Nugent actually joined Tattersalls a year before Richard, but was not appointed to the board until 1983. He is an auctioneer of immense experience as, apart from his work for Tattersalls, he sold for Goffs from 1955 to 1979 and also sold for Kells Livestock Mart for many years. He first sold for Tattersalls at the 1961 December Sales, but did not begin to sell regularly at Newmarket until four years later. He gives this account of his recall:

I was called back again for the December Sales in 1965 to cover for my great friend Bob Jeffares who, as a result of a fall on his head in a hunting accident, was suffering from double vision. We were not a very good team going over, as he could not see, and I was suffering from laryngitis and could not speak. However, Bob soldiered on for the first two or three days, at the end of which time he had to give up, and fortunately I had recovered my powers of speech.

Besides selling at Newmarket, the kind and genial Bob Jeffares was Tattersalls' agent in Ireland. When he died in 1973 at the age of only fifty-seven, his obituary in the *Bloodstock Breeders Review* contained this note on his auctioneering style:

Ever smiling, waving his gavel like a baton, his left hand almost invariably in his pocket, he possessed a persuasive, good-humoured rostrum manner.

Peter Nugent's style is more forceful than that of his great friend, and he injects an insistent sense of urgency into his selling. In addition to his work as an auctioneer, Bob Jeffares managed the Blackhall Stud at Clane in County Kildare for Lady Zia Wernher. After Bob died Peter succeeded him both as Tattersalls' Irish agent and as resident manager of the Blackhall Stud. He still held both those posts in 1986 when Edmond Mahony, the son of Tattersalls (Ireland) Ltd chairman Dennis Mahony, was assistant Tattersalls representative in Ireland.

The auctioneering partners have been supplemented at the main sales in recent years by the staff auctioneers Alan Taylor, Peter Holmes and Tony Chappell, and by David Pim and Edmond Mahony from Tattersalls (Ireland) – all thoroughly competent professionals. Alan Taylor retired at the age of sixty-five in 1985 after 38 years with the firm. To round off his career he was allotted the final stint of selling at the December Sales. He said afterwards: 'I was absolutely determined to sell the last lot through the ring, even though it had a 4000 guineas reserve on it and I had failed to sell the previous lot.' He easily achieved his object, as the bidding for the last lot, the three-year-old filly Transiberienne, reached 6800 guineas. At the fall of the hammer he was warmly applauded by the Tattersalls directors, bloodstock agents and friends who had gathered at the ringside to pay tribute to him.

Alan Taylor trained as an accountant before the Second

World War, but was in the army for more than six years during and after the war, in which he served with the Royal Corps of Signals in the North African and Italian campaigns. He joined Tattersalls in 1947, working in the accounts department at first, but soon moving into the bloodstock department. He succeeded to the post of office manager when Jack Cherry died in 1954, and held it until his retirement.

Alan's duties outside office management included the allocation of boxes for the sales and the production of the catalogues. The magnitude of the organization required to accommodate all the horses at the important sales is illustrated by the fact that at his last December Sales he had to make quadruple bookings for some of the boxes, in spite of the heavy building programme of the previous twenty years (the total reached 700 in 1986 with the completion of 70 new boxes at the Park Paddocks). Even more nightmarish were some of his past struggles to produce the catalogues in the days when the unions were able to exert a stranglehold and held the employers to ransom repeatedly. Alan always got them out on time, but sometimes it was a very close-run thing.

Brisk in manner, invariably courteous and never rattled, Alan Taylor was a corner-stone of the firm for many years. His dedication to a business which has made a substantial contribution to Britain's export earnings received well-merited recognition with the award of the MBE in 1975.

Peter Holmes is also a very long-serving member of the firm. He joined in 1948, just a year after Alan Taylor, and in the 1980s recalled with some amusement that his starting salary was £3 5s. a week. He first sold horses for Tattersalls at the July Sales in 1952, having been put through some arduous training sessions with Ken Watt and John Coventry acting as bidders. He must have made a good impression, because his first contract in May 1955 specified a greatly increased salary of £450 a year.

He had made a good impression, but not so good an impression that Ken Watt felt that he could be left unsupervised during his early months as an auctioneer. Ken was at his side while he was selling at the December Sales in 1952, until he glanced at his catalogue and saw that the next lot was Richer, who had won the Cambridgeshire two months earlier, with a 10,000 guineas reserve on him. 'He'll never make that. I can safely leave you', muttered Ken and departed from the

Alan Taylor, who was awarded the MBE in 1975, and Mrs Taylor receive a picture from the chairman, Michael Watt, at a ceremony to mark his retirement as Bloodstock Manager at the end of 1985

rostrum. Greatly to Peter's delight, he managed to extract precisely the reserve price for Richer, and knocked him down to the London Bloodstock Agency.

One night about that time a power cut plunged the sale ring into darkness while Peter was selling. The show had to go on, and selling proceeded with the ring illuminated by the headlights of the car which conveyed the staff between the Park Paddocks and the Rutland Arms, which was Tattersalls' Newmarket headquarters before the move from London.

Peter used to sell at Epsom during the short-lived sales there, and also used to sell occasionally at Goffs, then still at Ballsbridge, on an exchange basis with Peter Nugent. At the Ballsbridge yearling sales in 1963 he sold the colts who were to achieve fame as Meadow Court, winner of the Irish Sweeps Derby and the King George VI and Queen Elizabeth Stakes, and Hardicanute, winner of the Champagne Stakes and the Timeform Gold Cup. They were snapped up by that extremely good judge of a yearling, the Irish trainer Paddy Prendergast, for 3000 and 4700 guineas respectively. At the same sales nine years later he sold the colt by Ragusa out of the great broodmare Panaview for 40,000 guineas, then a record price for a yearling in Ireland. Named Ragapan, this colt had a somewhat chequered career on the racecourse, but did finish second in the Irish Sweeps Derby. In later years Peter became a more frequent visitor to Ireland as a director of Tattersalls (Ireland) Ltd.

These figures for his sales in Ireland were afterwards eclipsed in monetary, and indeed real, terms by some of his sales at Tattersalls. At the Premier Yearling Sales in 1981 he sold a colt by Alleged out of Foreign Missile, afterwards named Heron Bay, for 610,000 guineas, the second highest price of the year; and at the Highflyer Sales two years later he sold a colt by Thatching out of Miss Pudge, afterwards named Exhibitioner, for 420,000 guineas. They both went into Vincent O'Brien's stable and each won a Group 3 Pattern race, Heron Bay taking the Larkspur Stakes and Exhibitioner the Curragh Bloodstock Agency Greenlands Stakes.

At the Highflyer Sales in 1985 Peter sold the colt by Mill Reef out of Gift Wrapped for 600,000 guineas, the year's top price. Bluff and usually jovial, he commented a little ruefully: 'In the 1984 market he would have made a million.'

Undoubtedly one of the chief bulwarks of Tattersalls in the 1970s and 1980s was Geoffrey Hart. He had a well-established link with the Watts as a partner in the firm of Burton, Yeates and Hart, with offices in the Strand, who were solicitors to the Watt family. After some preliminary discussions, a letter from Michael Watt dated 6 November 1969 confirmed his appointment as 'financial consultant' to Tattersalls at a starting salary of £1500 a year. His title underestimated the range of his activities in Tattersalls' interests, as those activities rapidly expanded to embrace not only financial policy but legal advice in addition. Absolutely sound in both his advisory capacities and unswervingly loyal to the firm, he soon gained, and always kept, the complete confidence and friendship of the directors.

There could be no surer proof of faith in his judgement than the fact that at the beginning of the Lot 116 imbroglio, when Ken Watt was faced with the agonizing necessity to decide whether to re-auction immediately or resort to an alternative means of settling the crisis, it was Geoffrey Hart that he sent for to request the crucial interpretation of the Conditions of Sale: and then accepted his interpretation without question. It is highly significant that the final result of the case amounted to an endorsement of that interpretation.

One of Geoffrey Hart's heaviest responsibilities was the control of bad debts and all other problems associated with the credit-worthiness of Tattersalls' clients. Obviously there have always been, and always will be, some shady and untrustworthy characters on the disreputable fringes of the racing and breeding industry, attracted by the lure of easy money. Geoffrey had to keep a watchful eye on them. But his experience never bred an attitude of cynicism. On the contrary he found that the Turf was far from being the den of thieves that malevolent outsiders would like to paint it. Amazingly, in a business in which the exchange of huge sums of money depends on a barely perceptible nod or a minute wave of the catalogue, Tattersalls' bad debts have held steady at the remarkably low ratio of about £25 per £80,000 of turnover, while the standards of honesty in society as a whole have been in sharp decline.

Geoffrey Hart would be the best possible witness for the defence in any action impugning the integrity of the international thororoughbred breeding community.

The move of Tattersalls' main offices to Newmarket in 1977 was completely logical in commercial terms. It had not made sense to maintain an expensive administrative set-up at Knightsbridge Green in London, when all the firm's business was transacted 70 miles away, and concentration at Newmarket made for much greater convenience as well as savings. The new offices were established in Terrace House, which occupies a strategic position sandwiched between the Park Paddocks to the east and the High Street to the west, and at the same time the directors were able to acquire as their collective Newmarket residence Murray Lodge, a spacious red brick house set in beautiful gardens on higher ground to the south and commanding a view of the entire Park Paddocks complex. Murray Lodge provided the directors with not only comfortable accommodation for their increasingly lengthy stays in Newmarket, but also the facilities for entertaining friends and important clients. It was in every way a vast improvement on their previous cramped quarters at the Rutland Arms.

Terrace House was in a particular sense an appropriate location for Tattersalls' offices; for it was there that Reg Day, a great trainer of stayers, had prepared Solario to win the St Leger and the Ascot Gold Cup – and Solario had for many years held the record as the highest-priced horse ever sold by Tattersalls. A bonus was that the old trainer's yard at the back of the house provided useful additional boxes for the Park Paddocks.

Viewed in a wider context, the move may be seen as one facet of an epoch-making development in the history of British racing. Newmarket had long been known as the 'Headquarters of the Turf', and this title was justified by a number of facts: its two racecourses staged more days of flat racing than any other course in the country; its stables and training grounds accommodated more racehorses than any other training centre; there was a higher concentration of thoroughbred studs in the region than in any other part of Britain; the Jockey Club, though not its secretariat and administration, was located in the town; and the principal bloodstock sales were held in the Park Paddocks. But to a certain degree Newmarket had been out on a limb, divorced from many of the ancillary services which are essential for the efficient operation of a national thoroughbred industry. Tattersalls' office move was one step, and a very important step, in a progress towards rational centralization which, over a period of years, brought to Newmarket the National Stud as Britain's first large-scale stallion station, the Equine Research Station of the Animal Health Trust, many bloodstock agencies including the biggest, the BBA, the International Racing Bureau, insurance services, the offices of the Thoroughbred Breeders Association, the National Horseracing Museum and the British Racing School, and made the town a true headquarters offering comprehensive facilities to the industry.

Proximity facilitates cross-fertilization, and there is no doubt that the presence of the industry's principal institutions in Newmarket has promoted mutual cooperation and the growth of many of their most important functions. The same concentration has tended to increase awareness in the individual institutions of their responsibilities to the industry as a whole. In the case of Tattersalls this awareness has found practical expression in such measures as arranging the collection of the sales levy which helps to support veterinary research in Britain and Ireland, and an expanding programme of race sponsorship.

Race sponsorship serves two purposes: the self-interested purpose of direct advertisement of the firm, and the more altruistic purpose of promoting the prosperity of racing on which the commercial survival of every person and every organization involved in the industry ultimately depends. It is fair to assume that the former purpose was the sole inspiration of Tattersalls' first sponsorship of the Willesden Paddocks Stakes of 50 sovereigns each with 100 added by Tattersalls, run over the Rowley Mile at the Newmarket Craven Meeting in 1849. The Willesden Paddocks Stud, then situated in the County of Middlesex but now long since engulfed in the north-west suburbs of Greater London, was owned by Richard Tattersall, and entry to the race was restricted to three-year-olds sired by Elis, Sir Hercules, The Colonel or Ratcatcher, the stallions standing at the stud in 1844. Inevitably such restrictive conditions meant a small field, and in fact the three runners were all by Sir Hercules, the winner being the German Baron de Maltzahn's Armin, the favourite at 7–4 on.

Not surprisingly, the Willesden Paddocks Stakes was not repeated, and Tattersalls did not resume race sponsorship in Britain for thirty-two years. That indefatigable researcher Patrick Saward gave this account of the renewed sponsorship in a letter to Tattersalls' Public Relations Officer written in March 1975:

The Somerville Stakes, for two-year-olds sold by Messrs Tattersall as foals or yearlings, was first run at Newmarket, at the Second Spring Meeting, in 1880, with £300 added by the Jockey Club and £200 by Tattersalls. The Jockey Club contribution was dropped after 1899, but Tattersalls continued to sponsor the race, which in 1958 was re-named the Somerville Tattersall Stakes, with £1500 added.

Also in 1880, the Tattersall Sale Stakes was first run at Doncaster. . . . Ruff's Guide 1880, with conditions for the 1881 race, states it to be for two-year-olds 'sold by Messrs Tattersall the previous year'.

Clearly the motives of advertisement and sales promotion were uppermost in the staging of those races, but the emphasis began to shift after the Second World War with the extension of the race sponsorship base and the curtailment of the restrictions. However, the real explosion in Tattersalls' sponsorship occurred well after the move to Newmarket. By

1986 this sponsorship included two Group 1 two-year-old races, the Cheveley Park Stakes and the Middle Park Stakes, and the Group 3 Musidora Stakes, in England, and the Group 2 Tattersalls Rogers Gold Cup and the Group 3 Anglesey Stakes in Ireland, whose breeders have been making a substantial contribution to Tattersalls' business for more than a century. The Tattersalls Mares Only Novice Chase series, inaugurated in 1983, is an acknowledgement of the increased importance of the National Hunt side of the business, notably through the Tattersalls (Ireland) Derby Sale.

In 1986 Tattersalls' total race sponsorship amounted to £192,750, with no restrictive conditions – a sum which makes a striking contrast with the firm's tentative entry into sponsorship with the Willesden Park Stakes 138 years earlier.

In some senses the Tattersalls of old Richard and 'The Corner' seems infinitely remote from the Tattersalls of the Watts and the Park Paddocks. This aspect of the firm's historical development echoes T. S. Eliot's lines:

> I mount the steps and ring the bell, turning
> Wearily, as one would turn to nod goodbye to Rochefoucauld,
> If the street were time and he at the end of the street

Richard Tattersall plays Rochefoucauld to the non-Tattersalls who are the firm's directors in the last quarter of the twentieth century. But that is the founder seen through the wrong end of a telescope. Turn the telescope about and so much that seemed to be lost in the mists of time emerges in clear focus. In this way the modern observer can recognize much of the foundation that the first Tattersall laid – the honesty, the spirit of enterprise, the determination to hold the ring firmly and fairly between seller and buyer. All these are alive and still flourishing in the Tattersalls of the final quarter of the twentieth century.

Appendix I Winners of British Classic Races Sold by Tattersalls since 1920

Between 1920 and 1984 the winners of 74 British Classic races were sold at Tattersalls Sales:

2000 Guineas

St Louis, 1922
Diophon, 1924
Manna, 1925
Flamingo, 1928
Diolite, 1930
Orwell, 1932
Colombo, 1934
Kingsway, 1943
Nimbus, 1949
Ki-Ming, 1951
Nearula, 1953
Our Babu, 1955
Rockavon, 1961
Only For Life, 1963
Kashmir II, 1966
High Top, 1972 ★
Bolkonski, 1975
Wollow, 1976
Roland Gardens, 1978
To-Agori-Mou, 1981
Don't Forget Me, 1987

1000 Guineas

Four Course, 1931
Brown Betty, 1933
Musidora, 1949
Belle of All, 1951
Zabara, 1952
Happy Laughter, 1953
Sweet Solera, 1961
Pourparler, 1964
Glad Rags, 1966
Fleet, 1967
Humble Duty, 1970
Enstone Spark, 1978
One In A Million, 1979

Derby

Papyrus, 1923
Manna, 1925
Blenheim, 1930
April The Fifth, 1932
Windsor Lad, 1934
Mid-day Sun, 1937
Airborne, 1946
Nimbus, 1949
Pinza, 1953
Santa Claus, 1964
Snow Knight, 1974
Grundy, 1975

Oaks

Brownhylda, 1923
Straitlace, 1924
Rose of England, 1930
Chatelaine, 1933
Lovely Rosa, 1936
Musidora, 1949
Sweet Solera, 1961
Noblesse, 1963
Ginevra, 1972 ★
Fair Salinia, 1978
Circus Plume, 1984
Unite, 1987

St Leger

Salmon Trout, 1924
Solario, 1925
Singapore, 1930
Sandwich, 1931
Windsor Lad, 1934
Scottish Union, 1938
Chamossaire, 1945
Airborne, 1946
Sayajirao, 1947
Ridge Wood, 1949
Ballymoss, 1957
Aurelius, 1961
Indiana, 1964
Sodium, 1966
Athens Wood, 1971
Bustino, 1974
Bruni, 1975
Julio Mariner, 1978
Commanche Run, 1984

★ Bought privately – not included in sales totals.

Appendix II The Progress of Record Prices at Sales Conducted by Tattersalls

	Name	Price in guineas	Description
1872	Blair Athol	12,500	11-y-o stallion
1896	Meddler	14,500	3-y-o colt
1900	Flying Fox	37,500	4-y-o in training
1932	Solario	47,000	10-y-o stallion
1967	Vaguely Noble	136,000	2-y-o colt
1975	Filly by Mill Reef – Lalibela	202,000	yearling
1977	Colt by Lyphard – Chain	250,000	yearling
1978	Swiss Maid	325,000	3-y-o filly
1979	Colt by Lyphard – Swanilda	625,000	yearling
1981	Greenland Park	730,000	5-y-o mare in foal
1982	Tenea	1,020,000	3-y-o filly
1983	Colt by Hello Gorgeous – Centre Piece	1,550,000	yearling

INDEX